MznLnx

Missing Links Exam Preps

Exam Prep for

Cost Accounting: A Managerial Emphasis

Horngren, Datar & Foster, 12th Edition

The MznLnx Exam Prep is your link from the texbook and lecture to your exams.
The MznLnx Exam Preps are unauthorized and comprehensive reviews of your textbooks.

All material provided by MznLnx and Rico Publications (c) 2010
Textbook publishers and textbook authors do not particpate in or contribute to these reviews.

MznLnx

Rico
Publications

Exam Prep for Cost Accounting: A Managerial Emphasis
12th Edition
Horngren, Datar & Foster

Publisher: Raymond Houge
Assistant Editor: Michael Rouger
Text and Cover Designer: Lisa Buckner
Marketing Manager: Sara Swagger
Project Manager, Editorial Production: Jerry Emerson
Art Director: Vernon Lowerui

Product Manager: Dave Mason
Editorial Assitant: Rachel Guzmanji
Pedagogy: Debra Long
Cover Image: Jim Reed/Getty Images
Text and Cover Printer: City Printing, Inc.
Compositor: Media Mix, Inc.

(c) 2010 Rico Publications
ALL RIGHTS RESERVED. No part of this work covered by the copyright may be reproduced or used in any form or by an means--graphic, electronic, or mechanical, including photocopying, recording, taping, Web distribution, information storage, and retrieval systems, or in any other manner--without the written permission of the publisher.

For more information about our products, contact us at:

Dave.Mason@RicoPublications.com

For permission to use material from this text or

product, submit a request online to:

Dave.Mason@RicoPublications.com

Printed in the United States
ISBN:

Contents

CHAPTER 1
The Accountant's Role in the Organization   1

CHAPTER 2
An Introduction to Cost Terms and Purposes   12

CHAPTER 3
Cost-Volume-Profit Analysis   19

CHAPTER 4
Job Costing   24

CHAPTER 5
Activity-Based Costing and Activity-Based Management   28

CHAPTER 6
Master Budget and Responsibility Accounting   33

CHAPTER 7
Flexible Budgets, Direct-Cost Variances, and Management Control   41

CHAPTER 8
Flexible Budgets, Overhead Cost Variances, and Management Control   46

CHAPTER 9
Inventory Costing and Capacity Analysis   50

CHAPTER 10
Determining How Costs Behave   55

CHAPTER 11
Decision Making and Relevant Information   60

CHAPTER 12
Pricing Decisions and Cost Management   66

CHAPTER 13
Strategy, Balanced Scorecard, and Strategic Profitability Analysis   76

CHAPTER 14
Cost Allocation, Customer-Profitability Analysis, and Sales-Variance Analysis   81

CHAPTER 15
Allocation of Support-Department Costs, Common Costs and Revenues   84

CHAPTER 16
Cost Allocation: Joint Products and Byproducts   86

CHAPTER 17
Process Costing   88

CHAPTER 18
Spoilage, Rework, and Scrap   89

CHAPTER 19
Balanced Scorecard: Quality, Time, and the Theory of Constraints   91

CHAPTER 20
Inventory Management, Just-in-Time, and Backflush Costing   98

Contents (Cont.)

CHAPTER 21
Capital Budgeting and Cost Analysis — 104

CHAPTER 22
Management Control Systems, Transfer Pricing, and Multinational Considerations — 112

CHAPTER 23
Performance Measurement, Compensation, and Multinational Considerations — 117

ANSWER KEY — 124

TO THE STUDENT

COMPREHENSIVE

The *MznLnx* Exam Prep series is designed to help you pass your exams. Editors at MznLnx review your textbooks and then prepare these practice exams to help you master the textbook material. Unlike study guides, workbooks, and practice tests provided by the texbook publisher and textbook authors, *MznLnx* gives you **all** of the material in each chapter in exam form, not just samples, so you can be sure to nail your exam.

MECHANICAL

The MznLnx Exam Prep series creates exams that will help you learn the subject matter as well as test you on your understanding. Each question is designed to help you master the concept. Just working through the exams, you gain an understanding of the subject--its a simple mechanical process that produces success.

INTEGRATED STUDY GUIDE AND REVIEW

MznLnx is not just a set of exams designed to test you, its also a comprehensive review of the subject content. Each exam question is also a review of the concept, making sure that you will get the answer correct without having to go to other sources of material. You learn as you go! Its the easiest way to pass an exam.

HUMOR

Studying can be tedious and dry. MznLnx's instructional design includes moderate humor within the exam questions on occassion, to break the tedium and revitalize the brain

Chapter 1. The Accountant's Role in the Organization

1. An _____ is a practitioner of accountancy, which is the measurement, disclosure or provision of assurance about financial information that helps managers, investors, tax authorities and other decision makers make resource allocation decisions.

The word '_____' is derived from the French 'Compter' which took its origin from the Latin 'Computare'. The word was formerly written in English as 'Accomptant', but in process of time the word, which was always pronounced by dropping the 'p', became gradually changed both in pronunciation and in orthography to its present form.

   a. AIG
   b. ABC Television Network
   c. AMEX
   d. Accountant

2. In economics, business, retail, and accounting, a _____ is the value of money that has been used up to produce something, and hence is not available for use anymore. In economics, a _____ is an alternative that is given up as a result of a decision. In business, the _____ may be one of acquisition, in which case the amount of money expended to acquire it is counted as _____.
   a. Cost allocation
   b. Cost of quality
   c. Prime cost
   d. Cost

3. In management accounting, _____ establishes budget and actual cost of operations, processes, departments or product and the analysis of variances, profitability or social use of funds. Managers use _____ to support decision-making to cut a company's costs and improve profitability. As a form of management accounting, _____ need not follow standards such as GAAP, because its primary use is for internal managers, rather than outside users, and what to compute is instead decided pragmatically.
   a. Marginal cost
   b. Prime cost
   c. Cost accounting
   d. Cost-volume-profit analysis

4. _____ is the process whereby companies use cost accounting to report or control the various costs of doing business.

The term _____ is widely used in business today. Unfortunately _____ has no uniform definition.

a. Contribution margin
b. Process costing
c. Cost management
d. Contribution margin analysis

5. _____ is a repository of an organization's electronically stored data. _____s are designed to facilitate reporting and analysis.

This definition of the _____ focuses on data storage.

a. BNSF Railway
b. 3M Company
c. BMC Software, Inc.
d. Data warehouse

6. _____ is a company-wide computer software system used to manage and coordinate all the resources, information, and functions of a business from shared data stores.

An _____ system has a service-oriented architecture with modular hardware and software units or 'services' that communicate on a local area network. The modular design allows a business to add or reconfigure modules (perhaps from different vendors) while preserving data integrity in one shared database that may be centralized or distributed.

a. Enterprise Resource Planning
b. AMEX
c. ABC Television Network
d. AIG

7. _____ is the term used to refer to the standard framework of guidelines for financial accounting used in any given jurisdiction. _____ includes the standards, conventions, and rules accountants follow in recording and summarizing transactions, and in the preparation of financial statements.

Financial accounting information must be assembled and reported objectively.

a. Long-term liabilities
b. General ledger
c. Current asset
d. Generally accepted accounting principles

Chapter 1. The Accountant's Role in the Organization

8. _____ is a company's financial statement that indicates how the revenue is transformed into the net income The purpose of the _____ is to show managers and investors whether the company made or lost money during the period being reported.

The important thing to remember about an _____ is that it represents a period of time.

   a. ABC Television Network
   b. AMEX
   c. AIG
   d. Income statement

9. In economics, _____ is a rise in the general level of prices of goods and services in an economy over a period of time. When the general price level rises, each unit of currency buys fewer goods and services; consequently, _____ is also a decline in the real value of money--a loss of purchasing power in the medium of exchange which is also the monetary unit of account in the economy. A chief measure of general price-level _____ is the general _____ rate, which is the percentage change in a general price index (normally the Consumer Price Index) over time.
   a. Inflation
   b. Opportunity cost
   c. ABC Television Network
   d. AIG

10. _____ is concerned with the provisions and use of accounting information to managers within organizations, to provide them with the basis to make informed business decisions that will allow them to be better equipped in their management and control functions.

In contrast to financial accountancy information, _____ information is:

   - usually confidential and used by management, instead of publicly reported;
   - forward-looking, instead of historical;
   - pragmatically computed using extensive management information systems and internal controls, instead of complying with accounting standards.

This is because of the different emphasis: _____ information is used within an organization, typically for decision-making.

   a. Nonassurance services
   b. Management accounting
   c. Grenzplankostenrechnung
   d. Governmental accounting

Chapter 1. The Accountant's Role in the Organization

11. Government _____ are designed to show nonfinancial aspects of government operations. For example, a government financial report might include the number of arrests, number of convictions by crime category as well as the change (i.e., increase or decrease) in crime rate. Government _____ usually provide data on environmental conditions, education and conditions of streets and roads.

   a. BMC Software, Inc.
   b. BNSF Railway
   c. 3M Company
   d. Performance reports

12. In economics, _____ or _____ goods or real _____ refers to factors of production used to create goods or services that are not themselves significantly consumed (though they may depreciate) in the production process. _____ goods may be acquired with money or financial _____. In finance and accounting, _____ generally refers to financial wealth, especially that used to start or maintain a business.

   a. Capital
   b. Disclosure
   c. Vyborg Appeal
   d. Screening

13. _____ is the planning process used to determine whether a firm's long term investments such as new machinery, replacement machinery, new plants, new products, and research development projects are worth pursuing. It is budget for major capital, or investment, expenditures.

Many formal methods are used in _____, including the techniques such as

- Net present value
- Profitability index
- Internal rate of return
- Modified Internal Rate of Return
- Equivalent annuity

These methods use the incremental cash flows from each potential investment, or project. Techniques based on accounting earnings and accounting rules are sometimes used - though economists consider this to be improper - such as the accounting rate of return, and 'return on investment.' Simplified and hybrid methods are used as well, such as payback period and discounted payback period.

   a. Capital budgeting
   b. Gross profit
   c. Cash flow
   d. Preferred stock

Chapter 1. The Accountant's Role in the Organization 5

14. _____ is the balance of the amounts of cash being received and paid by a business during a defined period of time, sometimes tied to a specific project. Measurement of _____ can be used

- to evaluate the state or performance of a business or project.
- to determine problems with liquidity. Being profitable does not necessarily mean being liquid. A company can fail because of a shortage of cash, even while profitable.
- to project rate of returns. The time of _____s into and out of projects are used as inputs to financial models such as internal rate of return, and net present value.
- to examine income or growth of a business when it is believed that accrual accounting concepts do not represent economic realities. Alternately, _____ can be used to 'validate' the net income generated by accrual accounting.

_____ as a generic term may be used differently depending on context, and certain _____ definitions may be adapted by analysts and users for their own uses. Common terms include operating _____ and free _____.

 a. Controlling interest
 b. Cash flow
 c. Flow-through entity
 d. Commercial paper

15. A _____ is a commercial building for storage of goods. _____s are used by manufacturers, importers, exporters, wholesalers, transport businesses, customs, etc. They are usually large plain buildings in industrial areas of cities and towns.
 a. 3M Company
 b. BNSF Railway
 c. BMC Software, Inc.
 d. Warehouse

16. _____ is one of the four Ps of the marketing mix. The other three aspects are product, promotion, and place. It is also a key variable in microeconomic price allocation theory.
 a. Price
 b. Target costing
 c. Pricing
 d. Cost-plus pricing

17. A _____, also client, buyer or purchaser is the buyer or user of the paid products of an individual or organization, mostly called the supplier or seller. This is typically through purchasing or renting goods or services.

a. BMC Software, Inc.
b. BNSF Railway
c. 3M Company
d. Customer

18. _____ consists of the processes a company uses to track and organize its contacts with its current and prospective customers. _____ software is used to support these processes; information about customers and customer interactions can be entered, stored and accessed by employees in different company departments. Typical _____ goals are to improve services provided to customers, and to use customer contact information for targeted marketing.
  a. Customer relationship management
  b. Market share
  c. Market segmentation
  d. Value chain

19. _____ is a business management strategy aimed at embedding awareness of quality in all organizational processes. _____ has been widely used in manufacturing, education, call centers, government, and service industries, as well as NASA space and science programs.

When used together as a phrase, the three words in this expression have the following meanings:

- Total: Involving the entire organization, supply chain, and/or product life cycle
- Quality: With its usual definitions, with all its complexities
- Management: The system of managing with steps like Plan, Organize, Control, Lead, Staff, provisioning and organizing.

As defined by the International Organization for Standardization (ISO):

'_____ is a management approach for an organization, centered on quality, based on the participation of all its members and aiming at long-term success through customer satisfaction, and benefits to all members of the organization and to society.' ISO 8402:1994

One major aim is to reduce variation from every process so that greater consistency of effort is obtained. (Royse, D., Thyer, B., Padgett D., ' Logan T., 2006)

In Japan, _____ comprises four process steps, namely:

1. Kaizen - Focuses on 'Continuous Process Improvement', to make processes visible, repeatable and measurable.
2. Atarimae Hinshitsu - The idea that 'things will work as they are supposed to'.
3. Kansei - Examining the way the user applies the product leads to improvement in the product itself.
4. Miryokuteki Hinshitsu - The idea that 'things should have an aesthetic quality' (for example, a pen will write in a way that is pleasing to the writer.)

_____ requires that the company maintain this quality standard in all aspects of its business. This requires ensuring that things are done right the first time and that defects and waste are eliminated from operations.

a. BNSF Railway
b. BMC Software, Inc.
c. 3M Company
d. Total quality management

20. _____ is the process of comparing the cost, cycle time, productivity, or quality of a specific process or method to another that is widely considered to be an industry standard or best practice. Essentially, _____ provides a snapshot of the performance of your business and helps you understand where you are in relation to a particular standard. The result is often a business case for making changes in order to make improvements.
   a. BMC Software, Inc.
   b. Benchmarking
   c. Strategic business unit
   d. 3M Company

21. Project _____: The project _____ is a prediction of the costs associated with a particular company project. These costs include labor, materials, and other related expenses. The project _____ is often broken down into specific tasks, with task _____s assigned to each.
   a. 3M Company
   b. BNSF Railway
   c. BMC Software, Inc.
   d. Budget

22. _____ describes the situation when output from (or information about the result of) an event or phenomenon in the past will influence the same event/phenomenon in the present or future. When an event is part of a chain of cause-and-effect that forms a circuit or loop, then the event is said to 'feed back' into itself.

_____ is also a synonym for:

- _____ Signal; the information about the initial event that is the basis for subsequent modification of the event.
- _____ Loop; the causal path that leads from the initial generation of the _____ signal to the subsequent modification of the event.

_____ is a mechanism, process or signal that is looped back to control a system within itself. Such a loop is called a _____ loop.

a. Feedback
b. BMC Software, Inc.
c. Controllable
d. 3M Company

23. _____ is a demonstration of a process -- such as a variable, term, or object -- relative in terms of the specific process or set of validation tests used to determine its presence and quantity. Properties described in this manner must be sufficiently accessible, so that persons other than the definer may independently measure or test for them at will. An _____ is generally designed to model a conceptual definition.
a. AIG
b. AMEX
c. ABC Television Network
d. Operational definition

24. _____ is a term that refers both to:

- a formal discipline used to help appraise, or assess, the case for a project or proposal, which itself is a process known as project appraisal; and
- an informal approach to making decisions of any kind.

Under both definitions the process involves, whether explicitly or implicitly, weighing the total expected costs against the total expected benefits of one or more actions in order to choose the best or most profitable option. The formal process is often referred to as either CBA (_____) or BCost-benefit analysis

Chapter 1. The Accountant's Role in the Organization

A hallmark of CBA is that all benefits and all costs are expressed in money terms, and are adjusted for the time value of money, so that all flows of benefits and flows of project costs over time (which tend to occur at different points in time) are expressed on a common basis in terms of their 'e;present value.'e; Closely related, but slightly different, formal techniques include Cost-effectiveness analysis, Economic impact analysis, Fiscal impact analysis and Social Return on Investment(SROI) analysis. The latter builds upon the logic of _____, but differs in that it is explicitly designed to inform the practical decision-making of enterprise managers and investors focused on optimising their social and environmental impacts.

a. 3M Company
b. Cost-benefit analysis
c. BMC Software, Inc.
d. BNSF Railway

25. The _____ of a company or public agency is the corporate officer primarily responsible for managing the financial risks of the business or agency. This officer is also responsible for financial planning and record-keeping, as well as financial reporting to higher management. (In recent years, however, the role has expanded to encompass communicating financial performance and forecasts to the analyst community.)
  a. Chief financial officer
  b. Merck ' Co., Inc.
  c. Chief executive officer
  d. NASDAQ

26. A _____ or chief executive is one of the highest-ranking corporate officer (executive) or administrator in charge of total management. An individual selected as President and _____ of a corporation, company, organization, or agency, reports to the board of directors. In internal communication and press releases, many companies capitalize the term and those of other high positions, even when they are not proper nouns.
  a. Return on assets
  b. Return on equity
  c. Kohlberg Kravis Roberts ' Co
  d. Chief executive officer

27. An _____ is a term used in behavioral economics to describe those types of behaviors that impose costs on a person in the long-run that are not taken into account when making decisions in the present. Classical Economics discourages government from creating legislation that targets internalities, because it is assumed that the consumer takes these personal costs into account when paying for the good that causes the _____. For example, cigarettes should be taxed because of the negative consumption externalities that they impose, such as second-hand smoke, not because the smoker harms him or herself by smoking.

a. Authorised capital
b. Operating budget
c. Inventory turnover ratio
d. Internality

28. _____ is a strategic management responsibility that integrates finance, communication, marketing and securities law compliance to enable the most effective two-way communication between a company, the financial community, and other constituencies, which ultimately contributes to a company's securities achieving fair valuation. The term describes the department of a company devoted to handling inquiries from shareholders and investors, as well as others who might be interested in a company's stock or financial stability.
   a. AIG
   b. AMEX
   c. ABC Television Network
   d. Investor relations

29. _____ is a concept that denotes the precise probability of specific eventualities. Technically, the notion of _____ is independent from the notion of value and, as such, eventualities may have both beneficial and adverse consequences. However, in general usage the convention is to focus only on potential negative impact to some characteristic of value that may arise from a future event.
   a. Risk adjusted return on capital
   b. Discounting
   c. Discount factor
   d. Risk

30. The general definition of an _____ is an evaluation of a person, organization, system, process, project or product. _____s are performed to ascertain the validity and reliability of information; also to provide an assessment of a system's internal control. The goal of an _____ is to express an opinion on the person/organization/system (etc) in question, under evaluation based on work done on a test basis.
   a. Institute of Chartered Accountants of India
   b. Audit
   c. Assurance service
   d. Audit regime

31. A _____ is a group of employees from various functional areas of the organization - research, engineering, marketing, finance. human resources, and operations, for example - who are all focused on a specific objective and are responsible to work as a team to improve coordination and innovation across divisions and resolve mutual problems.

Chapter 1. The Accountant's Role in the Organization

a. Cross-functional team
b. BNSF Railway
c. BMC Software, Inc.
d. 3M Company

32. The _____ of 2002 (Pub.L. 107-204, 116 Stat. 745, enacted July 30, 2002), also known as the Public Company Accounting Reform and Investor Protection Act of 2002, is a United States federal law enacted on July 30, 2002 in response to a number of major corporate and accounting scandals including those affecting Enron, Tyco International, Adelphia, Peregrine Systems and WorldCom. The legislation establishes new or enhanced standards for all U.S. public company boards, management, and public accounting firms. It does not apply to privately held companies.

a. Lease
b. FCPA
c. Fair Labor Standards Act
d. Sarbanes-Oxley Act

33. The title _____ is a professional designation awarded by various professional bodies around the world.

The _____ designation is a post-nominal award issued to individuals who have achieved a peer-based criteria of professional competency in the field of Management Accounting. Management accounting qualifications differ from those such as the ACA or CPA 'Chartered' or 'Public' accounting qualifications in a number of ways.

a. Certified Management Accountant
b. BMC Software, Inc.
c. 3M Company
d. Convey Compliance Systems

34. The _____ is a professional organization headquartered in Montvale, New Jersey consisting of over 70,000 members worldwide. The IMA is dedicated to advancing the role of the management accountant and financial manager within the business organization, and provides relevant professional certification.

The IMA awards the Certified Management Accountant (CMA) designation in the United States.

a. Institute of Management Accountants
b. Emerging technologies
c. International Accounting Standards Committee
d. American Accounting Association

1. In economics, business, retail, and accounting, a _____ is the value of money that has been used up to produce something, and hence is not available for use anymore. In economics, a _____ is an alternative that is given up as a result of a decision. In business, the _____ may be one of acquisition, in which case the amount of money expended to acquire it is counted as _____.
   a. Cost allocation
   b. Cost
   c. Cost of quality
   d. Prime cost

2. _____ is a process of attributing cost to particular cost centres. For example the wage of the driver of the purchasing department can be allocated to the purchasing department cost centre. It is not necessary to share the wage cost over several different cost centers.
   a. Variable cost
   b. Cost allocation
   c. Cost of quality
   d. Cost accounting

3. A _____ is a tangible input for a product manufactured/Service provided, like labor or material. For example a cloth manufacturing firm requires some amount of predetermined labor and predetermined raw material for any amount of cloth being manufactured. The cost of employing labor can be directly fixed as 'per man per hour' or 'per man per day', so the labor is a _____ as you can directly associate cost with it.
   a. Residual value
   b. Round-tripping
   c. 3M Company
   d. Cost object

4. _____s are expenses that change in proportion to the activity of a business. In other words, _____ is the sum of marginal costs. It can also be considered normal costs.
   a. Cost accounting
   b. Quality costs
   c. Fixed costs
   d. Variable cost

5. _____ are costs that are not directly accountable to a particular function or product. _____ may be either fixed or variable. _____ include taxes, administration, personnel and security costs, and are also known as overhead.

a. Activity-based management
b. Indirect costs
c. Activity-based costing
d. ABC Television Network

6. In mathematics _____s are numbers or other things that get multiplied. In particular, see:

- Factorization, the decomposition of an object into a product of other objects
- Integer factorization, the process of breaking down a composite number into smaller non-trivial divisors
- A coefficient
- A divisor of a particular number, or of an element of a monoid
- A von Neumann algebra with a trivial center

In statistics

- _____ analysis is the study of how _____s or certain variables affect variables.

In technology:

- Human _____s, a profession that focuses on how people interact with products, tools, or procedures
- 'Functionality, Application domain, Conditions, Technology, Objects and Responsibility;', In object-oriented programming

In computer science and information technology:

- Authentication _____, a piece of information used to verify a person's identity for security purposes
- _____, a Unix command for numbers factorization
- _____ (programming language), an experimental Forth-like programming language

In television:

- The O'Reilly _____, an American talk show hosted by Bill O'Reilly on Fox News.
- The Krypton _____, a British game show hosted by Gordon Burns, formally on ITV. Also had an American version.

a. The Goodyear Tire ' Rubber Company
b. Valuation
c. Merck ' Co., Inc.
d. Factor

7. In economics, _____ are business expenses that are not dependent on the activities of the business They tend to be time-related, such as salaries or rents being paid per month. This is in contrast to variable costs, which are volume-related (and are paid per quantity.)

In management accounting, _____ are defined as expenses that do not change in proportion to the activity of a business, within the relevant period or scale of production.

   a. Cost accounting
   b. Cost of quality
   c. Marginal cost
   d. Fixed costs

8. A '_____' is the unit of an activity that causes the change of an activity cost. A _____ is any activity that causes a cost to be incurred. The Activity Based Costing (ABC) approach relates indirect cost to the activities that drive them to be incurred.
   a. Factory overhead
   b. Cost driver
   c. Contribution margin analysis
   d. Profit center

9. An _____ is a business that provides computer-based services to customers over a network. Software offered using an _____ model is also sometimes called On-demand software or software as a service (SaaS.) The most limited sense of this business is that of providing access to a particular application program (such as customer relationship management) using a standard protocol such as HTTP.
   a. AMEX
   b. Application Service Provider
   c. ABC Television Network
   d. AIG

10. Under the average-cost method, it is assumed that the cost of inventory is based on the _____ of the goods available for sale during the period. _____ is computed by dividing the total cost of goods available for sale by the total units available for sale. This gives a weighted-average unit cost that is applied to the units in the ending inventory.
   a. ABC Television Network
   b. AIG
   c. Ending inventory
   d. Average cost

Chapter 2. An Introduction to Cost Terms and Purposes

11. _____ is the total cost involved in operating all production facilities of a manufacturing business. It generally applies to indirect labor and indirect cost, it also includes all costs involved in manufacturing with the exception of the cost of raw materials and direct labor. _____ also includes certain costs such as quality assurance costs, cleanup costs, and property insurance premiums.

   a. Profit center
   b. Contribution margin analysis
   c. Cost driver
   d. Factory overhead

12. _____s are goods that have completed the manufacturing process but have not yet been sold or distributed to the end user.

Manufacturing has three classes of inventory:

   1. Raw material
   2. Work in process
   3. _____s

A good purchased as a 'raw material' goes into the manufacture of a product. A good only partially completed during the manufacturing process is called 'work in process'. When the good is completed as to manufacturing but not yet sold or distributed to the end-user is called a '_____'.

   a. FIFO and LIFO accounting
   b. Reorder point
   c. 3M Company
   d. Finished good

13. In business, _____, Overhead cost or _____ expense refers to an ongoing expense of operating a business. The term _____ is usually used to group expenses that are necessary to the continued functioning of the business, but do not directly generate profits.

_____ expenses are all costs on the income statement except for direct labor and direct materials.

   a. Overhead
   b. AIG
   c. ABC Television Network
   d. Intangible assets

14. _____ is the difference between operating revenues and operating expenses, but it is also sometimes used as a synonym for EBIT and operating profit. This is true if the firm has no non-_____.

Chapter 2. An Introduction to Cost Terms and Purposes

A professional investor contemplating a change to the capital structure of a firm first evaluates a firm's fundamental earnings potential (reflected by Earnings Before Interest, Taxes, Depreciation and Amortization EBITDA and EBIT), and then determines the optimal use of debt vs. equity.

a. AIG
b. ABC Television Network
c. AMEX
d. Operating income

15. A _____ is the pinnacle activity involved in selling products or services in return for money or other compensation. It is an act of completion of a commercial activity.

A _____ is completed by the seller, the owner of the goods.

a. High yield stock
b. Tertiary sector of economy
c. Maturity
d. Sale

16. _____ in engineering is a method of manufacturing in which the entire production process is controlled by computer. The traditional separated process methods are joined through a computer by CIM. This integration allows that the processes exchange information with each other and they are able to initiate actions.

a. BNSF Railway
b. Computer-integrated manufacturing
c. 3M Company
d. BMC Software, Inc.

17. Direct labor and overhead are often called conversion cost while direct material and direct labor are often referred to as _____.

For example, a manufacturing firm pays for raw materials. When activity is decreased, less raw material is used, and so the spending for raw materials falls.

a. Cost accounting
b. Marginal cost
c. Cost-volume-profit analysis
d. Prime cost

18. _____ is the amount of time someone works beyond normal working hours. Normal hours may be determined in several ways:

- by custom (what is considered healthy or reasonable by society),
- by practices of a given trade or profession,
- by legislation,
- by agreement between employers and workers or their representatives.

Most nations have _____ laws designed to dissuade or prevent employers from forcing their employees to work excessively long hours. These laws may take into account other considerations than the humanitarian, such as increasing the overall level of employment in the economy. One common approach to regulating _____ is to require employers to pay workers at a higher hourly rate for _____ work.

a. AMEX
b. ABC Television Network
c. AIG
d. Overtime

19. _____ are formal records of a business' financial activities.

In British English, including United Kingdom company law, _____ are often referred to as accounts, although the term _____ is also used, particularly by accountants.

_____ provide an overview of a business' financial condition in both short and long term.

a. 3M Company
b. Statement of retained earnings
c. Financial statements
d. Notes to the financial statements

20. _____ is the term used to refer to the standard framework of guidelines for financial accounting used in any given jurisdiction. _____ includes the standards, conventions, and rules accountants follow in recording and summarizing transactions, and in the preparation of financial statements.

Financial accounting information must be assembled and reported objectively.

a. Generally accepted accounting principles
b. General ledger
c. Current asset
d. Long-term liabilities

21. In management accounting, _____ establishes budget and actual cost of operations, processes, departments or product and the analysis of variances, profitability or social use of funds. Managers use _____ to support decision-making to cut a company's costs and improve profitability. As a form of management accounting, _____ need not follow standards such as GAAP, because its primary use is for internal managers, rather than outside users, and what to compute is instead decided pragmatically.
a. Prime cost
b. Cost-volume-profit analysis
c. Marginal cost
d. Cost accounting

22. _____ is the process whereby companies use cost accounting to report or control the various costs of doing business.

The term _____ is widely used in business today. Unfortunately _____ has no uniform definition.

a. Process costing
b. Contribution margin
c. Contribution margin analysis
d. Cost management

23. _____, in managerial economics is a form of cost accounting. It is a simplified model, useful for elementary instruction and for short-run decisions.

Cost-volume-profit (CVP) analysis expands the use of information provided by breakeven analysis.

a. Fixed costs
b. Cost of quality
c. Cost accounting
d. Cost-volume-profit analysis

Chapter 3. Cost-Volume-Profit Analysis

1. _____, in managerial economics is a form of cost accounting. It is a simplified model, useful for elementary instruction and for short-run decisions.

Cost-volume-profit (CVP) analysis expands the use of information provided by breakeven analysis.

   a. Fixed costs
   b. Cost accounting
   c. Cost-volume-profit analysis
   d. Cost of quality

2. In cost-volume-profit analysis, a form of management accounting, _____ is the marginal profit per unit sale. It is a useful quantity in carrying out various calculations, and can be used as a measure of operating leverage.

The Total _____ is Total Revenue (TR, or Sales) minus Total Variable Cost (TVC):

   Tcontribution margin = TR − TVC

The Unit _____ (C) is Unit Revenue (Price, P) minus Unit Variable Cost (V):

   C = P − V

The _____ Ratio is the percentage of Contribution over Total Revenue, which can be calculated from the unit contribution over unit price or total contribution over Total Revenue:

$$\frac{C}{P} = \frac{P-V}{P} = \frac{\text{Unit Contribution Margin}}{\text{Price}} = \frac{\text{Total Contribution Margin}}{\text{Total Revenue}}$$

For instance, if the price is $10 and the unit variable cost is $2, then the unit _____ is $8, and the _____ ratio is $8/$10 = 80%.

   a. Cost management
   b. Factory overhead
   c. Profit center
   d. Contribution margin

3. _____ is equal to the income that a firm has after subtracting costs and expenses from the total revenue. _____ can be distributed among holders of common stock as a dividend or held by the firm as retained earnings.

The items deducted will typically include tax expense, financing expense (interest expense), and minority interest. Likewise, preferred stock dividends will be subtracted too, though they are not an expense.

a. Net income
b. Long-term liabilities
c. Matching principle
d. Generally accepted accounting principles

4. A _____ is the pinnacle activity involved in selling products or services in return for money or other compensation. It is an act of completion of a commercial activity.

A _____ is completed by the seller, the owner of the goods.

a. Maturity
b. Tertiary sector of economy
c. High yield stock
d. Sale

5. _____ is a company's financial statement that indicates how the revenue is transformed into the net income The purpose of the _____ is to show managers and investors whether the company made or lost money during the period being reported.

The important thing to remember about an _____ is that it represents a period of time.

a. AMEX
b. AIG
c. Income statement
d. ABC Television Network

6. _____ is the difference between operating revenues and operating expenses, but it is also sometimes used as a synonym for EBIT and operating profit. This is true if the firm has no non-_____.

A professional investor contemplating a change to the capital structure of a firm first evaluates a firm's fundamental earnings potential (reflected by Earnings Before Interest, Taxes, Depreciation and Amortization EBITDA and EBIT), and then determines the optimal use of debt vs. equity.

a. AIG
b. ABC Television Network
c. AMEX
d. Operating income

Chapter 3. Cost-Volume-Profit Analysis 21

7. An _____ is a tax levied on the financial income of people, corporations, or other legal entities. Various _____ systems exist, with varying degrees of tax incidence. Income taxation can be progressive, proportional, or regressive.
   a. Income tax
   b. Individual Retirement Arrangement
   c. Implied level of government service
   d. Ordinary income

8. _____ can be regarded as an outcome of mental processes (cognitive process) leading to the selection of a course of action among several alternatives. Every _____ process produces a final choice. The output can be an action or an opinion of choice.
   a. BMC Software, Inc.
   b. BNSF Railway
   c. 3M Company
   d. Decision making

9. _____ is the study of how the variation (uncertainty) in the output of a mathematical model can be apportioned, qualitatively or quantitatively, to different sources of variation in the input of a model .

In more general terms uncertainty and sensitivity analyses investigate the robustness of a study when the study includes some form of mathematical modelling. While uncertainty analysis studies the overall uncertainty in the conclusions of the study, _____ tries to identify what source of uncertainty weights more on the study's conclusions.

   a. Sensitivity analysis
   b. Time to market
   c. Free cash flow
   d. Kaizen

10. _____ is a term used in subtly different ways in a number of fields, including philosophy, physics, statistics, economics, finance, insurance, psychology, sociology, engineering, and information science. It applies to predictions of future events, to physical measurements already made, or to the unknown.

In his seminal work Risk, _____, and Profit University of Chicago economist Frank Knight (1921) established the important distinction between risk and _____:

   ' _____ must be taken in a sense radically distinct from the familiar notion of risk, from which it has never been properly separated....

Chapter 3. Cost-Volume-Profit Analysis

a. AMEX
b. AIG
c. ABC Television Network
d. Uncertainty

11. In economics, business, retail, and accounting, a _____ is the value of money that has been used up to produce something, and hence is not available for use anymore. In economics, a _____ is an alternative that is given up as a result of a decision. In business, the _____ may be one of acquisition, in which case the amount of money expended to acquire it is counted as _____.
   a. Prime cost
   b. Cost of quality
   c. Cost allocation
   d. Cost

12. The _____ is a measure of how revenue growth translates into growth in operating income. It is a measure of leverage, and of how risky (volatile) a company's operating income is.

There are various measures of _____, which can be interpreted analogously to financial leverage.

   a. AlphaIC
   b. Upside potential ratio
   c. Information ratio
   d. Operating leverage

13. A '_____' is the unit of an activity that causes the change of an activity cost. A _____ is any activity that causes a cost to be incurred. The Activity Based Costing (ABC) approach relates indirect cost to the activities that drive them to be incurred.
   a. Contribution margin analysis
   b. Factory overhead
   c. Profit center
   d. Cost driver

14. _____, Gross profit margin or Gross Profit Rate can be defined as the amount of contribution to the business enterprise, after paying for direct-fixed and direct-variable unit costs, required to cover overheads (fixed commitments) and provide a buffer for unknown items. It expresses the relationship between gross profit and sales revenue.

It can be expressed in absolute terms:

Gross Profit = Revenue − Cost of Goods Sold

or as the ratio of gross profit to sales revenue, usually in the form of a percentage:

_____ Percentage = (Revenue-Cost of Goods Sold)/Revenue

Cost of goods sold includes variable costs and fixed costs directly linked to the product, such as material and labor.

a. Gross margin
b. BMC Software, Inc.
c. BNSF Railway
d. 3M Company

15. In probability theory and statistics, a _____ identifies either the probability of each value of an unidentified random variable (when the variable is discrete), or the probability of the value falling within a particular interval (when the variable is continuous.) The _____ describes the range of possible values that a random variable can attain and the probability that the value of the random variable is within any (measurable) subset of that range. The Normal distribution, often called the 'bell curve'

When the random variable takes values in the set of real numbers, the _____ is completely described by the cumulative distribution function, whose value at each real x is the probability that the random variable is smaller than or equal to x.

a. Time series
b. Moving average
c. Monte Carlo methods
d. Probability distribution

16. In probability theory and statistics, the _____ (or expectation value or mean and for continuous random variables with a density function it is the probability density -weighted integral of the possible values.

The term '_____' can be misleading.

a. AIG
b. AMEX
c. Expected value
d. ABC Television Network

Chapter 4. Job Costing

1. In economics, business, retail, and accounting, a _____ is the value of money that has been used up to produce something, and hence is not available for use anymore. In economics, a _____ is an alternative that is given up as a result of a decision. In business, the _____ may be one of acquisition, in which case the amount of money expended to acquire it is counted as _____.
   a. Cost of quality
   b. Cost allocation
   c. Prime cost
   d. Cost

2. _____ is a process of attributing cost to particular cost centres. For example the wage of the driver of the purchasing department can be allocated to the purchasing department cost centre. It is not necessary to share the wage cost over several different cost centers.
   a. Cost of quality
   b. Cost accounting
   c. Variable cost
   d. Cost allocation

3. A _____ is a tangible input for a product manufactured/Service provided, like labor or material. For example a cloth manufacturing firm requires some amount of predetermined labor and predetermined raw material for any amount of cloth being manufactured. The cost of employing labor can be directly fixed as 'per man per hour' or 'per man per day', so the labor is a _____ as you can directly associate cost with it.
   a. Cost object
   b. 3M Company
   c. Round-tripping
   d. Residual value

4. _____s are expenses that change in proportion to the activity of a business. In other words, _____ is the sum of marginal costs. It can also be considered normal costs.
   a. Fixed costs
   b. Quality costs
   c. Cost accounting
   d. Variable cost

5. _____ are costs that are not directly accountable to a particular function or product. _____ may be either fixed or variable. _____ include taxes, administration, personnel and security costs, and are also known as overhead.

Chapter 4. Job Costing

a. Indirect costs
b. ABC Television Network
c. Activity-based costing
d. Activity-based management

6. _____ is an accounting methodology that traces and accumulates direct costs, and allocates indirect costs of a manufacturing process. Costs are assigned to products, usually in a large batch, which might include an entire month's production. Eventually, costs have to be allocated to individual units of product.
   a. Cost management
   b. Profit center
   c. Cost driver
   d. Process Costing

7. _____ refers to the structured transmission of data between organizations by electronic means. It is used to transfer electronic documents from one computer system to another (ie) from one trading partner to another trading partner. It is more than mere E-mail; for instance, organizations might replace bills of lading and even checks with appropriate _____ messages.
   a. ABC Television Network
   b. AIG
   c. Electronic commerce
   d. Electronic Data Interchange

8. Government _____ are designed to show nonfinancial aspects of government operations. For example, a government financial report might include the number of arrests, number of convictions by crime category as well as the change (i.e., increase or decrease) in crime rate. Government _____ usually provide data on environmental conditions, education and conditions of streets and roads.
   a. 3M Company
   b. BNSF Railway
   c. Performance reports
   d. BMC Software, Inc.

9. The _____, sometimes known as the nominal ledger, is the main accounting record of a business which uses double-entry bookkeeping. It will usually include accounts for such items as current assets, fixed assets, liabilities, revenue and expense items, gains and losses.

The _____ is a collection of the group of accounts that supports the items shown in the major financial statements.

a. Journal entry
b. General journal
c. Sales journal
d. General ledger

10. A _____, in business matters, is an entity that is controlled by a bigger and more powerful entity. The controlled entity is called a company, corporation, or limited liability company, and the controlling entity is called its parent (or the parent company.) The reason for this distinction is that a lone company cannot be a _____ of any organization; only an entity representing a legal fiction as a separate entity can be a _____.

a. BMC Software, Inc.
b. Parent company
c. 3M Company
d. Subsidiary

11. The _____ is a subset of the general ledger used in accounting. The _____ shows detail for part of the accounting records such as property and equipment, prepaid expenses, etc. The detail would include such items as date the item was purchased or expense incurred, a description of the item, the original balance, and the net book value.

a. Minority interest
b. Subledger
c. Remittance advice
d. Credit memo

12. In business, _____, Overhead cost or _____ expense refers to an ongoing expense of operating a business. The term _____ is usually used to group expenses that are necessary to the continued functioning of the business, but do not directly generate profits.

_____ expenses are all costs on the income statement except for direct labor and direct materials.

a. Intangible assets
b. AIG
c. ABC Television Network
d. Overhead

13. _____ is an adverb or adjective, meaning in proportion. The term is used in many legal and economic contexts, and sometimes spelled pro-rata.

More specifically, _____ means:

1. In proportion to some factor that can be exactly calculated.
2. To count based on amount of time that has passed out of the total time.
3. Proportional Ratio

Pro-rata has a Latin etymology, from pro, according to, for, or by, and rata, feminine ablative of calculated.

Examples in law and economics include the following noted below.

a. BMC Software, Inc.
b. Pro rata
c. 3M Company
d. BNSF Railway

14. The term _____ describes a reduction in recognized value. In accounting terminology, it refers to recognition of the reduced or zero value of an asset. In income tax statements, it refers to a reduction of taxable income as recognition of certain expenses required to produce the income.
   a. Write-off
   b. Payroll
   c. Current asset
   d. Salvage value

15. In financial accounting, _____ or cost of sales includes the direct costs attributable to the production of the goods sold by a company. This amount includes the materials cost used in creating the goods along with the direct labor costs used to produce the good. It excludes indirect expenses such as distribution costs and sales force costs.
   a. FIFO and LIFO accounting
   b. Reorder point
   c. 3M Company
   d. Cost of goods sold

Chapter 5. Activity-Based Costing and Activity-Based Management

1. _____ is a costing model that identifies activities in an organization and assigns the cost of each activity resource to all products and services according to the actual consumption by each: it assigns more indirect costs (overhead) into direct costs.

In this way an organization can establish the true cost of its individual products and services for the purposes of identifying and eliminating those which are unprofitable and lowering the prices of those which are overpriced.

In a business organization, the ABC methodology assigns an organization's resource costs through activities to the products and services provided to its customers.

   a. Indirect costs
   b. Activity-based costing
   c. ABC Television Network
   d. Activity-based management

2. In economics, business, retail, and accounting, a _____ is the value of money that has been used up to produce something, and hence is not available for use anymore. In economics, a _____ is an alternative that is given up as a result of a decision. In business, the _____ may be one of acquisition, in which case the amount of money expended to acquire it is counted as _____.
   a. Cost of quality
   b. Prime cost
   c. Cost allocation
   d. Cost

3. _____ are costs that are not directly accountable to a particular function or product. _____ may be either fixed or variable. _____ include taxes, administration, personnel and security costs, and are also known as overhead.
   a. Activity-based management
   b. Activity-based costing
   c. ABC Television Network
   d. Indirect costs

4. _____ in engineering is a method of manufacturing in which the entire production process is controlled by computer. The traditional separated process methods are joined through a computer by CIM. This integration allows that the processes exchange information with each other and they are able to initiate actions.
   a. 3M Company
   b. BMC Software, Inc.
   c. BNSF Railway
   d. Computer-integrated manufacturing

Chapter 5. Activity-Based Costing and Activity-Based Management

5. _____ refers to the structured transmission of data between organizations by electronic means. It is used to transfer electronic documents from one computer system to another (ie) from one trading partner to another trading partner. It is more than mere E-mail; for instance, organizations might replace bills of lading and even checks with appropriate _____ messages.
   a. ABC Television Network
   b. Electronic Data Interchange
   c. Electronic commerce
   d. AIG

6. A _____ is a manufacturing system in which there is some amount of flexibility that allows the system to react in the case of changes, whether predicted or unpredicted. This flexibility is generally considered to fall into two categories, which both contain numerous subcategories.

The first category, machine flexibility, covers the system's ability to be changed to produce new product types, and ability to change the order of operations executed on a part.

   a. BNSF Railway
   b. 3M Company
   c. BMC Software, Inc.
   d. Flexible manufacturing system

7. Homogeneity means 'being similar throughout'.

Chapter 5. Activity-Based Costing and Activity-Based Management

Homogeneity may also refer to:

- _____, a variety of meanings
- In statistics homogeneity can refer to
    - Homogeneity of variance: Homoscedasticity
    - Logically consistent data matrices: homogeneity (statistics)
- Homogeneity (physics), in physics, two particular meanings: On one hand, translational invariance. On the other, homogeneity of units in equations, related to dimensional analysis
- Homogenetic or homoplastic, in biology, applied both to animals and plants, of having a resemblance in structure, due to descent from a common progenitor with subsequent modification
- Homogenization is intensive mixing of mutually insoluble phases (sometimes with addition of surfactants) to obtain a soluble suspension or emulsion, for example homogenizing milk so that the cream doesn't separate out
- In physical chemistry, _____ describes a single-phase system as opposed to a heterogeneous system. See also phase diagrams and the classification of catalysts
- In the context of procurement/purchasing, _____ is used to describe goods that do not vary in their essential characteristic irrespective of the source of supply

a. Homogeneous
b. Serial bonds
c. Scientific Research and Experimental Development Tax Incentive Program
d. Procter ' Gamble

8. A _____ is any one of a variety of different systems, institutions, procedures, social relations and infrastructures whereby persons trade, and goods and services are exchanged, forming part of the economy. It is an arrangement that allows buyers and sellers to exchange things. _____s vary in size, range, geographic scale, location, types and variety of human communities, as well as the types of goods and services traded.
a. Market Failure
b. Perfect competition
c. Recession
d. Market

9. _____ is the acquisition of goods and/or services at the best possible total cost of ownership, in the right quantity and quality, at the right time, in the right place and from the right source for the direct benefit or use of corporations or individuals, generally via a contract. Simple _____ may involve nothing more than repeat purchasing. Complex _____ could involve finding long term partners - or even 'co-destiny' suppliers that might fundamentally commit one organization to another.

Chapter 5. Activity-Based Costing and Activity-Based Management

a. Procurement
b. Time to market
c. Customer satisfaction
d. Free cash flow

10. _____ is the process whereby companies use cost accounting to report or control the various costs of doing business.

The term _____ is widely used in business today. Unfortunately _____ has no uniform definition.

a. Process costing
b. Cost management
c. Contribution margin analysis
d. Contribution margin

11. _____ is one of the four Ps of the marketing mix. The other three aspects are product, promotion, and place. It is also a key variable in microeconomic price allocation theory.
a. Cost-plus pricing
b. Price
c. Target costing
d. Pricing

12. _____ refers to the methods, practices and operations conducted to promote and sustain certain categories of commercial activity. The term is understood to have different specific meanings depending on the context. Merchandise is a sale goods at a store

In marketing, one of the definitions of _____ is the practice in which the brand or image from one product or service is used to sell another.

a. Merchandise
b. 3M Company
c. BMC Software, Inc.
d. Merchandising

13. _____ is a fee paid on borrowed assets. It is the price paid for the use of borrowed money , or, money earned by deposited funds .Assets that are sometimes lent with _____ include money, shares, consumer goods through hire purchase, major assets such as aircraft, and even entire factories in finance lease arrangements. The _____ is calculated upon the value of the assets in the same manner as upon money.

a. Insolvency
b. ABC Television Network
c. AIG
d. Interest

Chapter 6. Master Budget and Responsibility Accounting

1. Project _____: The project _____ is a prediction of the costs associated with a particular company project. These costs include labor, materials, and other related expenses. The project _____ is often broken down into specific tasks, with task _____s assigned to each.
   a. 3M Company
   b. BMC Software, Inc.
   c. BNSF Railway
   d. Budget

2. _____ is a Japanese philosophy that focuses on continuous improvement throughout all aspects of life. When applied to the workplace, _____ activities continually improve all functions of a business, from manufacturing to management and from the CEO to the assembly line workers. By improving standardized activities and processes, _____ aims to eliminate waste.
   a. Procurement
   b. Proprietorship
   c. Kaizen
   d. Sensitivity analysis

3. The term _____ is a term applied to practices that are perfunctory, or seek to satisfy the minimum requirements or to conform to a convention or doctrine. It has different meanings in different fields.

   In accounting, _____ earnings are those earnings of companies in addition to actual earnings calculated under the Generally Accepted Accounting Principles (GAAP) in their quarterly and yearly financial reports.

   a. Bottom line
   b. Payroll
   c. Treasury stock
   d. Pro forma

4. Employment is a contract between two parties, one being the employer and the other being the _____. An _____ may be defined as: 'A person in the service of another under any contract of hire, express or implied, oral or written, where the employer has the power or right to control and direct the _____ in the material details of how the work is to be performed.' Black's Law Dictionary page 471 (5th ed. 1979.)
   a. AMEX
   b. ABC Television Network
   c. Employee
   d. AIG

5. _____ refers to increasing the spiritual, political, social or economic strength of individuals and communities. It often involves the empowered developing confidence in their own capacities.

The term Human _____ covers a vast landscape of meanings, interpretations, definitions and disciplines ranging from psychology and philosophy to the highly commercialized Self-Help industry and Motivational sciences.

a. IMF
b. IPO
c. Entity
d. Empowerment

6. An _____ is the annual budget of an activity stated in terms of Budget Classification Code, functional/subfunctional categories and cost accounts. It contains estimates of the total value of resources required for the performance of the operation including reimbursable work or services for others. It also includes estimates of workload in terms of total work units identified by cost accounts.
a. Authorised capital
b. Inventory turnover ratio
c. Internality
d. Operating budget

7. In economics, business, retail, and accounting, a _____ is the value of money that has been used up to produce something, and hence is not available for use anymore. In economics, a _____ is an alternative that is given up as a result of a decision. In business, the _____ may be one of acquisition, in which case the amount of money expended to acquire it is counted as _____.
a. Prime cost
b. Cost allocation
c. Cost of quality
d. Cost

8. _____s are goods that have completed the manufacturing process but have not yet been sold or distributed to the end user.

Manufacturing has three classes of inventory:

1. Raw material
2. Work in process
3. _____s

A good purchased as a 'raw material' goes into the manufacture of a product. A good only partially completed during the manufacturing process is called 'work in process'. When the good is completed as to manufacturing but not yet sold or distributed to the end-user is called a '_____'.

a. Reorder point
b. FIFO and LIFO accounting
c. 3M Company
d. Finished good

9. _____ is a company's financial statement that indicates how the revenue is transformed into the net income The purpose of the _____ is to show managers and investors whether the company made or lost money during the period being reported.

The important thing to remember about an _____ is that it represents a period of time.

a. ABC Television Network
b. AMEX
c. AIG
d. Income statement

10. In business, _____, Overhead cost or _____ expense refers to an ongoing expense of operating a business. The term _____ is usually used to group expenses that are necessary to the continued functioning of the business, but do not directly generate profits.

_____ expenses are all costs on the income statement except for direct labor and direct materials.

a. AIG
b. ABC Television Network
c. Overhead
d. Intangible assets

11. _____ is the difference between operating revenues and operating expenses, but it is also sometimes used as a synonym for EBIT and operating profit. This is true if the firm has no non-_____.

A professional investor contemplating a change to the capital structure of a firm first evaluates a firm's fundamental earnings potential (reflected by Earnings Before Interest, Taxes, Depreciation and Amortization EBITDA and EBIT), and then determines the optimal use of debt vs. equity.

a. AMEX
b. ABC Television Network
c. AIG
d. Operating income

12. _____ refers to a business or organization attempting to acquire goods or services to accomplish the goals of the enterprise. Though there are several organizations that attempt to set standards in the _____ process, processes can vary greatly between organizations. Typically the word e;_____e; is not used interchangeably with the word e;procuremente;, since procurement typically includes Expediting, Supplier Quality, and Traffic and Logistics (T'L) in addition to _____.

a. Supply chain
b. Consignor
c. Purchasing
d. Free port

13. In financial accounting, _____ or cost of sales includes the direct costs attributable to the production of the goods sold by a company. This amount includes the materials cost used in creating the goods along with the direct labor costs used to produce the good. It excludes indirect expenses such as distribution costs and sales force costs.

a. Cost of goods sold
b. Reorder point
c. 3M Company
d. FIFO and LIFO accounting

14. _____ is the study of how the variation (uncertainty) in the output of a mathematical model can be apportioned, qualitatively or quantitatively, to different sources of variation in the input of a model.

In more general terms uncertainty and sensitivity analyses investigate the robustness of a study when the study includes some form of mathematical modelling. While uncertainty analysis studies the overall uncertainty in the conclusions of the study, _____ tries to identify what source of uncertainty weights more on the study's conclusions.

a. Free cash flow
b. Time to market
c. Kaizen
d. Sensitivity analysis

Chapter 6. Master Budget and Responsibility Accounting   37

15. _____ is a family of business models in which the buyer of a product provides certain information to a supplier of that product and the supplier takes full responsibility for maintaining an agreed inventory of the material, usually at the buyer's consumption location (usually a store.) A third party logistics provider can also be involved to make sure that the buyer have the required level of inventory by adjusting the demand and supply gaps.

As a symbiotic relationship, _____ makes it less likely that a business will unintentionally become out of stock of a good and reduces inventory in the supply chain.

   a. BMC Software, Inc.
   b. 3M Company
   c. Vendor Managed Inventory
   d. BNSF Railway

16. An _____ is a classification used for business units within an enterprise. The essential element of an _____ is that it is treated as a unit which is measured against its use of capital, as opposed to a cost or profit center, which are measured against raw costs or profits.

The advantage of this form of measurement is that it tends to be more encompassing, since it accounts for all uses of capital.

   a. AIG
   b. AMEX
   c. Investment center
   d. ABC Television Network

17. _____s are parts of a corporation that directly add to its profit.

A _____ manager is held accountable for both revenues, and costs (expenses), and therefore, profits. What this means in terms of managerial responsibilities is that the manager has to drive the sales revenue generating activities which leads to cash inflows and at the same time control the cost (cash outflows) causing activities.

   a. Cost management
   b. Profit center
   c. Cost driver
   d. Contribution margin

18. _____ is an important property of a control system, and the _____ property plays a crucial role in many control problems, such as stabilization of unstable systems by feedback, or optimal control.

_____ and observability are dual aspects of the same problem.

Roughly, the concept of _____ denotes the ability to move a system around in its entire configuration space using only certain admissible manipulations.

a. BMC Software, Inc.
b. 3M Company
c. Controllability
d. Controllable

19. _____ describes the situation when output from (or information about the result of) an event or phenomenon in the past will influence the same event/phenomenon in the present or future. When an event is part of a chain of cause-and-effect that forms a circuit or loop, then the event is said to 'feed back' into itself.

_____ is also a synonym for:

- _____ Signal; the information about the initial event that is the basis for subsequent modification of the event.
- _____ Loop; the causal path that leads from the initial generation of the _____ signal to the subsequent modification of the event.

_____ is a mechanism, process or signal that is looped back to control a system within itself. Such a loop is called a _____ loop.

a. 3M Company
b. BMC Software, Inc.
c. Controllable
d. Feedback

20. Government _____ are designed to show nonfinancial aspects of government operations. For example, a government financial report might include the number of arrests, number of convictions by crime category as well as the change (i.e., increase or decrease) in crime rate. Government _____ usually provide data on environmental conditions, education and conditions of streets and roads.

a. BMC Software, Inc.
b. BNSF Railway
c. 3M Company
d. Performance reports

Chapter 6. Master Budget and Responsibility Accounting

21. In probability theory and statistics, the _____ of a random variable, probability distribution averaging the squared distance of its possible values from the expected value (mean.) Whereas the mean is a way to describe the location of a distribution, the _____ is a way to capture its scale or degree of being spread out. The unit of _____ is the square of the unit of the original variable.
   a. Variance
   b. Time series
   c. Statistics
   d. Monte Carlo methods

22. An _____ is a practitioner of accountancy, which is the measurement, disclosure or provision of assurance about financial information that helps managers, investors, tax authorities and other decision makers make resource allocation decisions.

The word '_____' is derived from the French 'Compter' which took its origin from the Latin 'Computare'. The word was formerly written in English as 'Accomptant', but in process of time the word, which was always pronounced by dropping the 'p', became gradually changed both in pronunciation and in orthography to its present form.

   a. Accountant
   b. ABC Television Network
   c. AMEX
   d. AIG

23. _____ is concerned with the provisions and use of accounting information to managers within organizations, to provide them with the basis to make informed business decisions that will allow them to be better equipped in their management and control functions.

In contrast to financial accountancy information, _____ information is:

  - usually confidential and used by management, instead of publicly reported;
  - forward-looking, instead of historical;
  - pragmatically computed using extensive management information systems and internal controls, instead of complying with accounting standards.

This is because of the different emphasis: _____ information is used within an organization, typically for decision-making.

a. Grenzplankostenrechnung
b. Governmental accounting
c. Management accounting
d. Nonassurance services

Chapter 7. Flexible Budgets, Direct-Cost Variances, and Management Control

1. _____ is a Japanese philosophy that focuses on continuous improvement throughout all aspects of life. When applied to the workplace, _____ activities continually improve all functions of a business, from manufacturing to management and from the CEO to the assembly line workers. By improving standardized activities and processes, _____ aims to eliminate waste .
   a. Procurement
   b. Sensitivity analysis
   c. Proprietorship
   d. Kaizen

2. _____ is a 'policy by which management devotes its time to investigating only those situations in which actual results differ significantly from planned results. The idea is that management should spend its valuable time concentrating on the more important items (such as shaping the company's future strategic course.) Attention is given only to material deviations requiring investigation.'

   It is not entirely synonymous with the concept of exception management in that it describes a policy where absolute focus is on exception management, in contrast to moderate application of exception management.

   a. Performance measurement
   b. Cash cow
   c. Best practice
   d. Management by exception

3. In probability theory and statistics, the _____ of a random variable, probability distribution averaging the squared distance of its possible values from the expected value (mean.) Whereas the mean is a way to describe the location of a distribution, the _____ is a way to capture its scale or degree of being spread out. The unit of _____ is the square of the unit of the original variable.
   a. Monte Carlo methods
   b. Variance
   c. Time series
   d. Statistics

4. Project _____: The project _____ is a prediction of the costs associated with a particular company project. These costs include labor, materials, and other related expenses. The project _____ is often broken down into specific tasks, with task _____s assigned to each.
   a. BMC Software, Inc.
   b. BNSF Railway
   c. 3M Company
   d. Budget

Chapter 7. Flexible Budgets, Direct-Cost Variances, and Management Control

5. _____ in economics and business is the result of an exchange and from that trade we assign a numerical monetary value to a good, service or asset. If Alice trades Bob 4 apples for an orange, the _____ of an orange is 4 apples. Inversely, the _____ of an apple is 1/4 oranges.
   a. Transactional Net Margin Method
   b. Discounts and allowances
   c. Price discrimination
   d. Price

6. The materials _____ is computed as follows:

   Vmp = (Actual Unit Cost - Standard Unit Cost) * Actual Quantity Purchased

or

   Vmp = (Actual Quantity Purchased * Actual Unit Cost) - (Actual Quantity Purchased * Standard Unit Cost.)

When the Actual Materials Price is higher than the Standard Materials Price, the variance is said to be unfavorable, since the Actual price paid on materials purchased is greater than the allowed standard. The variance is said to be favorable when the Standard materials Price is higher than the Actual Materials Price, since less money was spent in purchasing the materials than the allowed standard.

   a. Fund accounting
   b. Liquidating dividend
   c. Consolidated financial statements
   d. Price variance

7. In economics, business, retail, and accounting, a _____ is the value of money that has been used up to produce something, and hence is not available for use anymore. In economics, a _____ is an alternative that is given up as a result of a decision. In business, the _____ may be one of acquisition, in which case the amount of money expended to acquire it is counted as _____.
   a. Prime cost
   b. Cost
   c. Cost allocation
   d. Cost of quality

Chapter 7. Flexible Budgets, Direct-Cost Variances, and Management Control

8. A _____ has several related meanings:

   - a daily record of events or business; a private _____ is usually referred to as a diary.
   - a newspaper or other periodical, in the literal sense of one published each day;
   - many publications issued at stated intervals, such as magazines, or scholarly academic _____s, or the record of the transactions of a society, are often called _____s. Although _____ is sometimes used, erroneously, as a synonym for 'magazine,' in academic use, a _____ refers to a serious, scholarly publication, most often peer-reviewed. A non-scholarly magazine written for an educated audience about an industry or an area of professional activity is usually called a professional magazine.

The word 'journalist' for one whose business is writing for the public press has been in use since the end of the 17th century.

Open access _____s are scholarly _____s that are available to the reader without financial or other barrier other than access to the internet itself. Some are subsidized, and some require payment on behalf of the author. Subsidized _____s are financed by an academic institution or a government information center.

   a. BMC Software, Inc.
   b. BNSF Railway
   c. 3M Company
   d. Journal

9. _____ refers to the structured transmission of data between organizations by electronic means. It is used to transfer electronic documents from one computer system to another (ie) from one trading partner to another trading partner. It is more than mere E-mail; for instance, organizations might replace bills of lading and even checks with appropriate _____ messages.
   a. Electronic Data Interchange
   b. AIG
   c. Electronic commerce
   d. ABC Television Network

10. _____ is the process whereby an organization establishes the parameters within which programs, investments, and acquisitions are reaching the desired results. Performance Reference Model of the Federal Enterprise Architecture, 2005.

This process of measuring performance often requires the use of statistical evidence to determine progress toward specific defined organizational objectives.

There are many types of measurements.

a. Performance measurement
b. Management by exception
c. Trustee
d. Management by objectives

11. Total _____ is a method of Accounting cost which entails the full cost of manufacturing or providing a service. This includes not just the costs of materials and labour, but also of all manufacturing overheads (whether e;fixede; or e;variablee;.) One of the main reasons for absorbing overheads into the cost of units is for inventory valuation purposes.

a. ABC Television Network
b. Absorption costing
c. AMEX
d. AIG

12. _____ Process Deming saw it as part of the 'system' whereby feedback from the process and customer were evaluated against organisational goals.

a. Sensitivity analysis
b. Sole proprietorship
c. Procurement
d. Continuous improvement

13. _____ is a costing model that identifies activities in an organization and assigns the cost of each activity resource to all products and services according to the actual consumption by each: it assigns more indirect costs (overhead) into direct costs.

In this way an organization can establish the true cost of its individual products and services for the purposes of identifying and eliminating those which are unprofitable and lowering the prices of those which are overpriced.

In a business organization, the ABC methodology assigns an organization's resource costs through activities to the products and services provided to its customers.

a. ABC Television Network
b. Activity-based management
c. Activity-based costing
d. Indirect costs

Chapter 7. Flexible Budgets, Direct-Cost Variances, and Management Control

14. In statistics, _____ (ANOVA) is a collection of statistical models, and their associated procedures, in which the observed variance is partitioned into components due to different explanatory variables. In its simplest form ANOVA gives a statistical test of whether the means of several groups are all equal, and therefore generalizes Student's two-sample t-test to more than two groups.

There are three conceptual classes of such models:

1. Fixed-effects models assumes that the data came from normal populations which may differ only in their means. (Model 1)
2. Random effects models assume that the data describe a hierarchy of different populations whose differences are constrained by the hierarchy. (Model 2)
3. Mixed-effect models describe situations where both fixed and random effects are present. (Model 3)

In practice, there are several types of ANOVA depending on the number of treatments and the way they are applied to the subjects in the experiment:

- One-way ANOVA is used to test for differences among two or more independent groups. Typically, however, the one-way ANOVA is used to test for differences among at least three groups, since the two-group case can be covered by a T-test (Gossett, 1908.)

a. IMF
b. Analysis of variance
c. Open database connectivity
d. Intergenerational equity

15. _____ is the process of comparing the cost, cycle time, productivity, or quality of a specific process or method to another that is widely considered to be an industry standard or best practice. Essentially, _____ provides a snapshot of the performance of your business and helps you understand where you are in relation to a particular standard. The result is often a business case for making changes in order to make improvements.
a. Benchmarking
b. BMC Software, Inc.
c. 3M Company
d. Strategic business unit

Chapter 8. Flexible Budgets, Overhead Cost Variances, and Management Control

1. In economics, business, retail, and accounting, a _____ is the value of money that has been used up to produce something, and hence is not available for use anymore. In economics, a _____ is an alternative that is given up as a result of a decision. In business, the _____ may be one of acquisition, in which case the amount of money expended to acquire it is counted as _____.
   a. Cost of quality
   b. Cost allocation
   c. Cost
   d. Prime cost

2. A _____ has several related meanings:

   - a daily record of events or business; a private _____ is usually referred to as a diary.
   - a newspaper or other periodical, in the literal sense of one published each day;
   - many publications issued at stated intervals, such as magazines, or scholarly academic _____s, or the record of the transactions of a society, are often called _____s. Although _____ is sometimes used, erroneously, as a synonym for 'magazine,' in academic use, a _____ refers to a serious, scholarly publication, most often peer-reviewed. A non-scholarly magazine written for an educated audience about an industry or an area of professional activity is usually called a professional magazine.

   The word 'journalist' for one whose business is writing for the public press has been in use since the end of the 17th century.

   Open access _____s are scholarly _____s that are available to the reader without financial or other barrier other than access to the internet itself. Some are subsidized, and some require payment on behalf of the author. Subsidized _____s are financed by an academic institution or a government information center.

   a. BNSF Railway
   b. Journal
   c. BMC Software, Inc.
   d. 3M Company

3. In business, _____, Overhead cost or _____ expense refers to an ongoing expense of operating a business. The term _____ is usually used to group expenses that are necessary to the continued functioning of the business, but do not directly generate profits.

   _____ expenses are all costs on the income statement except for direct labor and direct materials.

   a. AIG
   b. Intangible assets
   c. Overhead
   d. ABC Television Network

Chapter 8. Flexible Budgets, Overhead Cost Variances, and Management Control

4. Project _____: The project _____ is a prediction of the costs associated with a particular company project. These costs include labor, materials, and other related expenses. The project _____ is often broken down into specific tasks, with task _____s assigned to each.
   a. Budget
   b. BNSF Railway
   c. BMC Software, Inc.
   d. 3M Company

5. In probability theory and statistics, the _____ of a random variable, probability distribution averaging the squared distance of its possible values from the expected value (mean.) Whereas the mean is a way to describe the location of a distribution, the _____ is a way to capture its scale or degree of being spread out. The unit of _____ is the square of the unit of the original variable.
   a. Statistics
   b. Monte Carlo methods
   c. Time series
   d. Variance

6. _____ is a common concept in economics, and gives rise to derived concepts such as consumer debt. Generally _____ is defined by opposition to production. But the precise definition can vary because different schools of economists define production quite differently.
   a. Mitigating Control
   b. Yield
   c. Starving the beast
   d. Consumption

7. _____ is an overall management philosophy introduced by Dr. Eliyahu M. Goldratt in his 1984 book titled The Goal, that is geared to help organizations continually achieve their goal. The title comes from the contention that any manageable system is limited in achieving more of its goal by a very small number of constraints, and that there is always at least one constraint. The _____ process seeks to identify the constraint and restructure the rest of the organization around it, through the use of the Five Focusing Steps.
   a. Six Sigma
   b. Lean manufacturing
   c. Lean production
   d. Theory of constraints

Chapter 8. Flexible Budgets, Overhead Cost Variances, and Management Control

8. In statistics, _____ (ANOVA) is a collection of statistical models, and their associated procedures, in which the observed variance is partitioned into components due to different explanatory variables. In its simplest form ANOVA gives a statistical test of whether the means of several groups are all equal, and therefore generalizes Student's two-sample t-test to more than two groups.

There are three conceptual classes of such models:

1. Fixed-effects models assumes that the data came from normal populations which may differ only in their means. (Model 1)
2. Random effects models assume that the data describe a hierarchy of different populations whose differences are constrained by the hierarchy. (Model 2)
3. Mixed-effect models describe situations where both fixed and random effects are present. (Model 3)

In practice, there are several types of ANOVA depending on the number of treatments and the way they are applied to the subjects in the experiment:

- One-way ANOVA is used to test for differences among two or more independent groups. Typically, however, the one-way ANOVA is used to test for differences among at least three groups, since the two-group case can be covered by a T-test (Gossett, 1908.)

a. Analysis of variance
b. Open database connectivity
c. Intergenerational equity
d. IMF

9. _____ is one of the four Ps of the marketing mix. The other three aspects are product, promotion, and place. It is also a key variable in microeconomic price allocation theory.
a. Price
b. Pricing
c. Target costing
d. Cost-plus pricing

10. _____ is a costing model that identifies activities in an organization and assigns the cost of each activity resource to all products and services according to the actual consumption by each: it assigns more indirect costs (overhead) into direct costs.

In this way an organization can establish the true cost of its individual products and services for the purposes of identifying and eliminating those which are unprofitable and lowering the prices of those which are overpriced.

In a business organization, the ABC methodology assigns an organization's resource costs through activities to the products and services provided to its customers.

a. Indirect costs
b. Activity-based costing
c. ABC Television Network
d. Activity-based management

Chapter 9. Inventory Costing and Capacity Analysis

1. Total _____ is a method of Accounting cost which entails the full cost of manufacturing or providing a service. This includes not just the costs of materials and labour, but also of all manufacturing overheads (whether e;fixede; or e;variablee;.) One of the main reasons for absorbing overheads into the cost of units is for inventory valuation purposes.

    a. AMEX
    b. ABC Television Network
    c. AIG
    d. Absorption costing

2. _____s are expenses that change in proportion to the activity of a business. In other words, _____ is the sum of marginal costs. It can also be considered normal costs.

    a. Quality costs
    b. Cost accounting
    c. Fixed costs
    d. Variable cost

3. In economics, business, retail, and accounting, a _____ is the value of money that has been used up to produce something, and hence is not available for use anymore. In economics, a _____ is an alternative that is given up as a result of a decision. In business, the _____ may be one of acquisition, in which case the amount of money expended to acquire it is counted as _____.

    a. Prime cost
    b. Cost allocation
    c. Cost of quality
    d. Cost

4. _____ is a company's financial statement that indicates how the revenue is transformed into the net income The purpose of the _____ is to show managers and investors whether the company made or lost money during the period being reported.

    The important thing to remember about an _____ is that it represents a period of time.

    a. AIG
    b. AMEX
    c. ABC Television Network
    d. Income statement

5. _____ is the difference between operating revenues and operating expenses, but it is also sometimes used as a synonym for EBIT and operating profit. This is true if the firm has no non-_____.

Chapter 9. Inventory Costing and Capacity Analysis 51

A professional investor contemplating a change to the capital structure of a firm first evaluates a firm's fundamental earnings potential (reflected by Earnings Before Interest, Taxes, Depreciation and Amortization EBITDA and EBIT), and then determines the optimal use of debt vs. equity.

a. ABC Television Network
b. AIG
c. AMEX
d. Operating income

6. A _____ is the pinnacle activity involved in selling products or services in return for money or other compensation. It is an act of completion of a commercial activity.

A _____ is completed by the seller, the owner of the goods.

a. Tertiary sector of economy
b. Maturity
c. High yield stock
d. Sale

7. _____ is the process whereby an organization establishes the parameters within which programs, investments, and acquisitions are reaching the desired results. Performance Reference Model of the Federal Enterprise Architecture, 2005.

This process of measuring performance often requires the use of statistical evidence to determine progress toward specific defined organizational objectives.

There are many types of measurements.

a. Management by objectives
b. Management by exception
c. Performance measurement
d. Trustee

8. _____ is systematic determination of merit, worth, and significance of something or someone using criteria against a set of standards. _____ often is used to characterize and appraise subjects of interest in a wide range of human enterprises, including the arts, criminal justice, foundations and non-profit organizations, government, health care, and other human services.

Chapter 9. Inventory Costing and Capacity Analysis

Depending on the topic of interest, there are professional groups which look to the quality and rigor of the _____ process.

a. ABC Television Network
b. AIG
c. AMEX
d. Evaluation

9. _____ is a concept in economics which refers to the extent to which an enterprise or a nation actually uses its installed productive capacity. Thus, it refers to the relationship between actual output that 'is' produced with the installed equipment and the potential output which 'could' be produced with it, if capacity was fully used.

If market demand grows, _____ will rise.

a. Long-run
b. 3M Company
c. BMC Software, Inc.
d. Capacity utilization

10. _____ is a process used to manage information technology (IT). Its primary goal is to ensure that IT capacity meets current and future business requirements in a cost-effective manner. One common interpretation of _____ is described in the ITIL framework. ITIL version 3 views _____ as comprising three sub-processes: business _____, service _____, and component _____.

a. 3M Company
b. BMC Software, Inc.
c. BNSF Railway
d. Capacity management

11. _____ is an adverb or adjective, meaning in proportion. The term is used in many legal and economic contexts, and sometimes spelled pro-rata.

More specifically, _____ means:

1. In proportion to some factor that can be exactly calculated.
2. To count based on amount of time that has passed out of the total time.
3. Proportional Ratio

Pro-rata has a Latin etymology, from pro, according to, for, or by, and rata, feminine ablative of calculated .

Examples in law and economics include the following noted below.

a. 3M Company
b. BMC Software, Inc.
c. Pro rata
d. BNSF Railway

12. The term _____ describes a reduction in recognized value. In accounting terminology, it refers to recognition of the reduced or zero value of an asset. In income tax statements, it refers to a reduction of taxable income as recognition of certain expenses required to produce the income.

a. Salvage value
b. Write-off
c. Payroll
d. Current asset

13. In financial accounting, _____ or cost of sales includes the direct costs attributable to the production of the goods sold by a company. This amount includes the materials cost used in creating the goods along with the direct labor costs used to produce the good. It excludes indirect expenses such as distribution costs and sales force costs.

a. FIFO and LIFO accounting
b. Cost of goods sold
c. Reorder point
d. 3M Company

14. In probability theory and statistics, the _____ of a random variable, probability distribution averaging the squared distance of its possible values from the expected value (mean.) Whereas the mean is a way to describe the location of a distribution, the _____ is a way to capture its scale or degree of being spread out. The unit of _____ is the square of the unit of the original variable.

a. Variance
b. Monte Carlo methods
c. Time series
d. Statistics

15. _____ is the process of estimation in unknown situations. Prediction is a similar, but more general term. Both can refer to estimation of time series, cross-sectional or longitudinal data.

a. Forecasting
b. BNSF Railway
c. 3M Company
d. BMC Software, Inc.

Chapter 10. Determining How Costs Behave

1. In economics, business, retail, and accounting, a _____ is the value of money that has been used up to produce something, and hence is not available for use anymore. In economics, a _____ is an alternative that is given up as a result of a decision. In business, the _____ may be one of acquisition, in which case the amount of money expended to acquire it is counted as _____.
   a. Prime cost
   b. Cost allocation
   c. Cost of quality
   d. Cost

2. A '_____' is the unit of an activity that causes the change of an activity cost. A _____ is any activity that causes a cost to be incurred. The Activity Based Costing (ABC) approach relates indirect cost to the activities that drive them to be incurred.
   a. Profit center
   b. Cost driver
   c. Contribution margin analysis
   d. Factory overhead

3. _____ is an area of engineering practice concerned with the 'application of scientific principles and techniques to problems of cost estimating, cost control, business planning and management science, profitability analysis, project management, and planning and scheduling.'

   Key objectives of _____ are to arrive at accurate cost estimates and to avoid cost overruns. The broad array of _____ topics represent the intersection of the fields of project management, business management, and engineering. Most people have a limited view of what engineering encompasses.

   a. 3M Company
   b. BMC Software, Inc.
   c. BNSF Railway
   d. Cost engineering

4. _____ is the calculated approximation of a result which is usable even if input data may be incomplete or uncertain.

   In statistics, see _____ theory, estimator.

   In mathematics, approximation or _____ typically means finding upper or lower bounds of a quantity that cannot readily be computed precisely and is also an educated guess.

a. AIG
b. ABC Television Network
c. AMEX
d. Estimation

5. _____ or cross section (of a study population) in statistics and econometrics is a type of one-dimensional data set. _____ refers to data collected by observing many subjects (such as individuals, firms or countries/regions) at the same point of time, or without regard to differences in time. Analysis of _____ usually consists of comparing the differences among the subjects.
   a. BMC Software, Inc.
   b. BNSF Railway
   c. 3M Company
   d. Cross-sectional data

6. In statistics, signal processing, and many other fields, a _____ is a sequence of data points, measured typically at successive times, spaced at (often uniform) time intervals. _____ analysis comprises methods that attempt to understand such _____, often either to understand the underlying context of the data points (Where did they come from? What generated them?), or to make forecasts (predictions.) _____ forecasting is the use of a model to forecast future events based on known past events: to forecast future data points before they are measured.
   a. Statistics
   b. Variance
   c. Moving average
   d. Time series

7. In statistics, _____ refers to techniques for the modeling and analysis of numerical data consisting of values of a dependent variable and of one or more independent variables The dependent variable in the regression equation is modeled as a function of the independent variables, corresponding parameters, and an error term. The error term is treated as a random variable.
   a. Trend analysis
   b. 3M Company
   c. Multicollinearity
   d. Regression analysis

8. The _____ of a statistical model describes how well it fits a set of observations. Measures of _____ typically summarize the discrepancy between observed values and the values expected under the model in question. Such measures can be used in statistical hypothesis testing, e.g. to test for normality of residuals, to test whether two samples are drawn from identical distributions , or whether outcome frequencies follow a specified distribution

Chapter 10. Determining How Costs Behave

a. BMC Software, Inc.
b. Goodness of fit
c. 3M Company
d. BNSF Railway

9. The terms 'dependent variable' and '_____' are used in similar but subtly different ways in mathematics and statistics as part of the standard terminology in those subjects. They are used to distinguish between two types of quantities being considered, separating them into those available at the start of a process and those being created by it, where the latter (dependent variables) are dependent on the former (_____s.)

In traditional calculus, a function is defined as a relation between two terms called variables because their values vary.

a. ABC Television Network
b. AMEX
c. Independent variable
d. AIG

10. _____ is a costing model that identifies activities in an organization and assigns the cost of each activity resource to all products and services according to the actual consumption by each: it assigns more indirect costs (overhead) into direct costs.

In this way an organization can establish the true cost of its individual products and services for the purposes of identifying and eliminating those which are unprofitable and lowering the prices of those which are overpriced.

In a business organization, the ABC methodology assigns an organization's resource costs through activities to the products and services provided to its customers.

a. Activity-based management
b. Indirect costs
c. ABC Television Network
d. Activity-based costing

11. Models of the learning curve effect and the closely related _____ effect express the relationship between equations for experience and efficiency or between efficiency gains and investment in the effort. The experience of 'learning curves' was first observed by the 19th Century German psychologist Hermann Ebbinghaus according to the difficulty of memorizing varying numbers of verbal stimuli, and subsequent learning about the complex processes of learning are discussed in the

The rule used for representing the learning curve effect states that the more times a task has been performed, the less time will be required on each subsequent iteration.

a. AMEX
b. AIG
c. ABC Television Network
d. Experience curve

12. Models of the _____ effect and the closely related experience curve effect express the relationship between equations for experience and efficiency or between efficiency gains and investment in the effort. The experience of '_____s' was first observed by the 19th Century German psychologist Hermann Ebbinghaus according to the difficulty of memorizing varying numbers of verbal stimuli, and subsequent learning about the complex processes of learning are discussed in the

The rule used for representing the _____ effect states that the more times a task has been performed, the less time will be required on each subsequent iteration.

a. Learning curve
b. 3M Company
c. Strategic business unit
d. BMC Software, Inc.

13. In statistics, the _____, R^2 is used in the context of statistical models whose main purpose is the prediction of future outcomes on the basis of other related information. It is the proportion of variability in a data set that is accounted for by the statistical model. It provides a measure of how well future outcomes are likely to be predicted by the model.
a. Trend analysis
b. Regression analysis
c. 3M Company
d. Coefficient of determination

14. _____ is a statistical phenomenon in which two or more predictor variables in a multiple regression model are highly correlated. In this situation the coefficient estimates may change erratically in response to small changes in the model or the data. _____ does not reduce the predictive power or reliability of the model as a whole; it only affects calculations regarding individual predictors.

a. 3M Company
b. Trend analysis
c. Multicollinearity
d. Regression analysis

Chapter 11. Decision Making and Relevant Information

1. _____ is one of the four Ps of the marketing mix. The other three aspects are product, promotion, and place. It is also a key variable in microeconomic price allocation theory.
   a. Price
   b. Pricing
   c. Target costing
   d. Cost-plus pricing

2. In economics, business, retail, and accounting, a _____ is the value of money that has been used up to produce something, and hence is not available for use anymore. In economics, a _____ is an alternative that is given up as a result of a decision. In business, the _____ may be one of acquisition, in which case the amount of money expended to acquire it is counted as _____.
   a. Cost
   b. Prime cost
   c. Cost of quality
   d. Cost allocation

3. In economics and business decision-making, _____ are costs that cannot be recovered once they have been incurred. _____ are sometimes contrasted with variable costs, which are the costs that will change due to the proposed course of action, and prospective costs which are costs that will be incurred if an action is taken.

In traditional microeconomic theory, only variable costs are relevant to a decision.

   a. BMC Software, Inc.
   b. Sunk costs
   c. BNSF Railway
   d. 3M Company

4. In mathematics _____s are numbers or other things that get multiplied. In particular, see:

   - Factorization, the decomposition of an object into a product of other objects
   - Integer factorization, the process of breaking down a composite number into smaller non-trivial divisors
   - A coefficient
   - A divisor of a particular number, or of an element of a monoid
   - A von Neumann algebra with a trivial center

In statistics

   - _____ analysis is the study of how _____s or certain variables affect variables.

Chapter 11. Decision Making and Relevant Information

In technology:

- Human _____s, a profession that focuses on how people interact with products, tools, or procedures
- 'Functionality, Application domain, Conditions, Technology, Objects and Responsibility;', In object-oriented programming

In computer science and information technology:

- Authentication _____, a piece of information used to verify a person's identity for security purposes
- _____, a Unix command for numbers factorization
- _____ (programming language), an experimental Forth-like programming language

In television:

- The O'Reilly _____, an American talk show hosted by Bill O'Reilly on Fox News.
- The Krypton _____, a British game show hosted by Gordon Burns, formally on ITV. Also had an American version.

a. Merck ' Co., Inc.
b. Valuation
c. The Goodyear Tire ' Rubber Company
d. Factor

5. _____ accounting (Full costA) generally refers to the process of collecting and presenting information (costs as well as advantages) for each proposed alternative when a decision is necessary. A synonym, true cost accounting (TCA) is also often used. Experts consider both terms problematic as definitions of 'true' and 'full' are inherently subjective
   a. BNSF Railway
   b. Full cost
   c. 3M Company
   d. BMC Software, Inc.

6. _____ is subcontracting a process, such as product design or manufacturing, to a third-party company. The decision to outsource is often made in the interest of lowering cost or making better use of time and energy costs, redirecting or conserving energy directed at the competencies of a particular business, or to make more efficient use of land, labor, capital, (information) technology and resources. _____ became part of the business lexicon during the 1980s.

a. Outsourcing
b. US Airways, Inc.
c. USA Today
d. Economic Growth and Tax Relief Reconciliation Act of 2001

7. In economics and finance, _____ is the change in total cost that arises when the quantity produced changes by one unit. It is the cost of producing one more unit of a good. Mathematically, the _____ function is expressed as the first derivative of the total cost (TC) function with respect to quantity (Q.)
   a. Cost accounting
   b. Cost of quality
   c. Variable cost
   d. Marginal cost

8. _____ describes the relocation by a company of a business process from one country to another -- typically an operational process such as manufacturing, or supporting processes, such as accounting. Even state governments employ _____.
   a. AMEX
   b. Offshoring
   c. AIG
   d. ABC Television Network

9. _____ or economic opportunity loss is the value of the next best alternative foregone as the result of making a decision. _____ analysis is an important part of a company's decision-making processes but is not treated as an actual cost in any financial statement. The next best thing that a person can engage in is referred to as the _____ of doing the best thing and ignoring the next best thing to be done.
   a. Inflation
   b. AIG
   c. Opportunity cost
   d. ABC Television Network

10. A _____, also client, buyer or purchaser is the buyer or user of the paid products of an individual or organization, mostly called the supplier or seller. This is typically through purchasing or renting goods or services.
    a. Customer
    b. BMC Software, Inc.
    c. 3M Company
    d. BNSF Railway

Chapter 11. Decision Making and Relevant Information

11. In economics, _____ or _____ goods or real _____ refers to factors of production used to create goods or services that are not themselves significantly consumed (though they may depreciate) in the production process. _____ goods may be acquired with money or financial _____. In finance and accounting, _____ generally refers to financial wealth, especially that used to start or maintain a business.
    a. Capital
    b. Vyborg Appeal
    c. Disclosure
    d. Screening

12. _____ is the planning process used to determine whether a firm's long term investments such as new machinery, replacement machinery, new plants, new products, and research development projects are worth pursuing. It is budget for major capital, or investment, expenditures.

    Many formal methods are used in _____, including the techniques such as

    - Net present value
    - Profitability index
    - Internal rate of return
    - Modified Internal Rate of Return
    - Equivalent annuity

    These methods use the incremental cash flows from each potential investment, or project. Techniques based on accounting earnings and accounting rules are sometimes used - though economists consider this to be improper - such as the accounting rate of return, and 'return on investment.' Simplified and hybrid methods are used as well, such as payback period and discounted payback period.

    a. Cash flow
    b. Gross profit
    c. Preferred stock
    d. Capital budgeting

13. In accounting, _____ or carrying value is the value of an asset according to its balance sheet account balance. For assets, the value is based on the original cost of the asset less any depreciation, amortization or impairment costs made against the asset. Traditionally, a company's _____ is its total assets minus intangible assets and liabilities.
    a. Generally accepted accounting principles
    b. Depreciation
    c. Matching principle
    d. Book value

14. _____ is systematic determination of merit, worth, and significance of something or someone using criteria against a set of standards. _____ often is used to characterize and appraise subjects of interest in a wide range of human enterprises, including the arts, criminal justice, foundations and non-profit organizations, government, health care, and other human services.

Depending on the topic of interest, there are professional groups which look to the quality and rigor of the _____ process.

    a. Evaluation
    b. AMEX
    c. AIG
    d. ABC Television Network

15. An _____ is a practitioner of accountancy, which is the measurement, disclosure or provision of assurance about financial information that helps managers, investors, tax authorities and other decision makers make resource allocation decisions.

The word '_____' is derived from the French 'Compter' which took its origin from the Latin 'Computare'. The word was formerly written in English as 'Accomptant', but in process of time the word, which was always pronounced by dropping the 'p', became gradually changed both in pronunciation and in orthography to its present form.

    a. AIG
    b. AMEX
    c. ABC Television Network
    d. Accountant

16. _____ is concerned with the provisions and use of accounting information to managers within organizations, to provide them with the basis to make informed business decisions that will allow them to be better equipped in their management and control functions.

In contrast to financial accountancy information, _____ information is:

- usually confidential and used by management, instead of publicly reported;
- forward-looking, instead of historical;
- pragmatically computed using extensive management information systems and internal controls, instead of complying with accounting standards.

This is because of the different emphasis: _____ information is used within an organization, typically for decision-making.

a. Management accounting
b. Nonassurance services
c. Grenzplankostenrechnung
d. Governmental accounting

17. In mathematics, _____ is a technique for optimization of a linear objective function, subject to linear equality and linear inequality constraints. Informally, _____ determines the way to achieve the best outcome (such as maximum profit or lowest cost) in a given mathematical model and given some list of requirements represented as linear equations.

More formally, given a polytope (for example, a polygon or a polyhedron), and a real-valued affine function

$$f(x_1, x_2, \ldots, x_n) = c_1 x_1 + c_2 x_2 + \cdots + c_n x_n + d$$

defined on this polytope, a _____ method will find a point in the polytope where this function has the smallest (or largest) value.

a. BNSF Railway
b. 3M Company
c. BMC Software, Inc.
d. Linear programming

18. _____ is the study of how the variation (uncertainty) in the output of a mathematical model can be apportioned, qualitatively or quantitatively, to different sources of variation in the input of a model.

In more general terms uncertainty and sensitivity analyses investigate the robustness of a study when the study includes some form of mathematical modelling. While uncertainty analysis studies the overall uncertainty in the conclusions of the study, _____ tries to identify what source of uncertainty weights more on the study's conclusions.

a. Free cash flow
b. Kaizen
c. Time to market
d. Sensitivity analysis

Chapter 12. Pricing Decisions and Cost Management

1. _____ is one of the four Ps of the marketing mix. The other three aspects are product, promotion, and place. It is also a key variable in microeconomic price allocation theory.
   a. Price
   b. Cost-plus pricing
   c. Target costing
   d. Pricing

2. A _____ is a fixed point of time in the future at which point certain processes will be evaluated or assumed to end. It is necessary in an accounting, finance or risk management regime to assign such a fixed horizon time so that alternatives can be evaluated for performance over the same period of time. A _____ is a physical impossibility in the real world.
   a. 3M Company
   b. BMC Software, Inc.
   c. BNSF Railway
   d. Time horizon

3. In economics, business, retail, and accounting, a _____ is the value of money that has been used up to produce something, and hence is not available for use anymore. In economics, a _____ is an alternative that is given up as a result of a decision. In business, the _____ may be one of acquisition, in which case the amount of money expended to acquire it is counted as _____.
   a. Cost allocation
   b. Prime cost
   c. Cost
   d. Cost of quality

4. In economics, the concept of the _____ refers to the decision-making time frame of a firm in which at least one factor of production is fixed. Costs which are fixed in the _____ have no impact on a firms decisions. For example a firm can raise output by increasing the amount of labour through overtime.
   a. 3M Company
   b. Long-run
   c. BMC Software, Inc.
   d. Short-run

Chapter 12. Pricing Decisions and Cost Management

5. In mathematics _____s are numbers or other things that get multiplied. In particular, see:

- Factorization, the decomposition of an object into a product of other objects
- Integer factorization, the process of breaking down a composite number into smaller non-trivial divisors
- A coefficient
- A divisor of a particular number, or of an element of a monoid
- A von Neumann algebra with a trivial center

In statistics

- _____ analysis is the study of how _____s or certain variables affect variables.

In technology:

- Human _____s, a profession that focuses on how people interact with products, tools, or procedures
- 'Functionality, Application domain, Conditions, Technology, Objects and Responsibility;', In object-oriented programming

In computer science and information technology:

- Authentication _____, a piece of information used to verify a person's identity for security purposes
- _____, a Unix command for numbers factorization
- _____ (programming language), an experimental Forth-like programming language

In television:

- The O'Reilly _____, an American talk show hosted by Bill O'Reilly on Fox News.
- The Krypton _____, a British game show hosted by Gordon Burns, formally on ITV. Also had an American version.

a. The Goodyear Tire ' Rubber Company
b. Merck ' Co., Inc.
c. Factor
d. Valuation

6. _____ is a costing model that identifies activities in an organization and assigns the cost of each activity resource to all products and services according to the actual consumption by each: it assigns more indirect costs (overhead) into direct costs.

In this way an organization can establish the true cost of its individual products and services for the purposes of identifying and eliminating those which are unprofitable and lowering the prices of those which are overpriced.

In a business organization, the ABC methodology assigns an organization's resource costs through activities to the products and services provided to its customers.

a. Activity-based management
b. Indirect costs
c. ABC Television Network
d. Activity-based costing

7. In economic models, the _____ time frame assumes no fixed factors of production. Firms can enter or leave the marketplace, and the cost (and availability) of land, labor, raw materials, and capital goods can be assumed to vary. In contrast, in the short-run time frame, certain factors are assumed to be fixed, because there is not sufficient time for them to change.
a. 3M Company
b. Short-run
c. BMC Software, Inc.
d. Long-run

8. A _____ is an economy based on the division of labor in which the prices of goods and services are determined in a free price system set by supply and demand. This is often contrasted with a planned economy, in which a central government determines the price of goods and services using a fixed price system. Market economies are contrasted with mixed economy where the price system is not entirely free but under some government control that is not extensive enough to constitute a planned economy.
a. 3M Company
b. Market economy
c. BNSF Railway
d. BMC Software, Inc.

9. A _____ is any one of a variety of different systems, institutions, procedures, social relations and infrastructures whereby persons trade, and goods and services are exchanged, forming part of the economy. It is an arrangement that allows buyers and sellers to exchange things. _____s vary in size, range, geographic scale, location, types and variety of human communities, as well as the types of goods and services traded.
a. Market Failure
b. Perfect competition
c. Market
d. Recession

Chapter 12. Pricing Decisions and Cost Management

10. _____ in marketing and strategic management is an assessment of the strengths and weaknesses of current and potential competitors. This analysis provides both an offensive and defensive strategic context through which to identify opportunities and threats. Competitor profiling coalesces all of the relevant sources of _____ into one framework in the support of efficient and effective strategy formulation, implementation, monitoring and adjustment.
    a. 3M Company
    b. BNSF Railway
    c. BMC Software, Inc.
    d. Competitor analysis

11. A _____, also client, buyer or purchaser is the buyer or user of the paid products of an individual or organization, mostly called the supplier or seller. This is typically through purchasing or renting goods or services.
    a. Customer
    b. BMC Software, Inc.
    c. 3M Company
    d. BNSF Railway

12. _____ is a pricing method used by firms. It is defined as 'a cost management tool for reducing the overall cost of a product over its entire life-cycle with the help of production, engineering, research and design'. A target cost is the maximum amount of cost that can be incurred on a product and with it the firm can still earn the required profit margin from that product at a particular selling price.
    a. Discounts and allowances
    b. Pricing
    c. Penetration pricing
    d. Target costing

13. In economics, _____ or _____ goods or real _____ refers to factors of production used to create goods or services that are not themselves significantly consumed (though they may depreciate) in the production process. _____ goods may be acquired with money or financial _____. In finance and accounting, _____ generally refers to financial wealth, especially that used to start or maintain a business.
    a. Screening
    b. Disclosure
    c. Vyborg Appeal
    d. Capital

14. _____ is the planning process used to determine whether a firm's long term investments such as new machinery, replacement machinery, new plants, new products, and research development projects are worth pursuing. It is budget for major capital, or investment, expenditures.

Many formal methods are used in _____, including the techniques such as

- Net present value
- Profitability index
- Internal rate of return
- Modified Internal Rate of Return
- Equivalent annuity

These methods use the incremental cash flows from each potential investment, or project. Techniques based on accounting earnings and accounting rules are sometimes used - though economists consider this to be improper - such as the accounting rate of return, and 'return on investment.' Simplified and hybrid methods are used as well, such as payback period and discounted payback period.

a. Gross profit
b. Preferred stock
c. Cash flow
d. Capital budgeting

15. _____ is the difference between operating revenues and operating expenses, but it is also sometimes used as a synonym for EBIT and operating profit. This is true if the firm has no non-_____.

A professional investor contemplating a change to the capital structure of a firm first evaluates a firm's fundamental earnings potential (reflected by Earnings Before Interest, Taxes, Depreciation and Amortization EBITDA and EBIT), and then determines the optimal use of debt vs. equity.

a. ABC Television Network
b. AMEX
c. AIG
d. Operating income

16. _____ is a systematic method to improve the 'value' of goods or products and services by using an examination of function. Value, as defined, is the ratio of function to cost. Value can therefore be increased by either improving the function or reducing the cost.
a. Value engineering
b. Changeover
c. Productivity
d. Deming Prize

Chapter 12. Pricing Decisions and Cost Management

17. _____ refers to the additional value of a commodity over the cost of commodities used to produce it from the previous stage of production. An example is the price of gasoline at the pump over the price of the oil in it. In national accounts used in macroeconomics, it refers to the contribution of the factors of production, i.e., land, labor, and capital goods, to raising the value of a product and corresponds to the incomes received by the owners of these factors.
   a. Value added
   b. Minimum wage
   c. 3M Company
   d. Supply-side economics

18. A _____ is a group of employees from various functional areas of the organization - research, engineering, marketing, finance. human resources, and operations, for example - who are all focused on a specific objective and are responsible to work as a team to improve coordination and innovation across divisions and resolve mutual problems.
   a. BMC Software, Inc.
   b. 3M Company
   c. Cross-functional team
   d. BNSF Railway

19. An _____ is a practitioner of accountancy, which is the measurement, disclosure or provision of assurance about financial information that helps managers, investors, tax authorities and other decision makers make resource allocation decisions.

The word '_____' is derived from the French 'Compter' which took its origin from the Latin 'Computare'. The word was formerly written in English as 'Accomptant', but in process of time the word, which was always pronounced by dropping the 'p', became gradually changed both in pronunciation and in orthography to its present form.

   a. AIG
   b. Accountant
   c. AMEX
   d. ABC Television Network

20. _____ Process Deming saw it as part of the 'system' whereby feedback from the process and customer were evaluated against organisational goals.
   a. Continuous improvement
   b. Procurement
   c. Sole proprietorship
   d. Sensitivity analysis

Chapter 12. Pricing Decisions and Cost Management

21. _____ is a Japanese philosophy that focuses on continuous improvement throughout all aspects of life. When applied to the workplace, _____ activities continually improve all functions of a business, from manufacturing to management and from the CEO to the assembly line workers. By improving standardized activities and processes, _____ aims to eliminate waste .
   a. Proprietorship
   b. Kaizen
   c. Sensitivity analysis
   d. Procurement

22. _____ is concerned with the provisions and use of accounting information to managers within organizations, to provide them with the basis to make informed business decisions that will allow them to be better equipped in their management and control functions.

In contrast to financial accountancy information, _____ information is:

- usually confidential and used by management, instead of publicly reported;
- forward-looking, instead of historical;
- pragmatically computed using extensive management information systems and internal controls, instead of complying with accounting standards.

This is because of the different emphasis: _____ information is used within an organization, typically for decision-making.

   a. Grenzplankostenrechnung
   b. Governmental accounting
   c. Nonassurance services
   d. Management accounting

23. In finance, _____ also known as return on investment, rate of profit or sometimes just return, is the ratio of money gained or lost on an investment relative to the amount of money invested. The amount of money gained or lost may be referred to as interest, profit/loss, gain/loss, or net income/loss. The money invested may be referred to as the asset, capital, principal, or the cost basis of the investment.
   a. Theoretical ex-rights price
   b. Debt to capital ratio
   c. Capital employed
   d. Rate of return

24. _____ is a pricing method used by companies. It is used primarily because it is easy to calculate and requires little information. There are several varieties, but the common thread in all of them is that one first calculates the cost of the product, then includes an additional amount to represent profit.

Chapter 12. Pricing Decisions and Cost Management

a. Penetration pricing
b. Target costing
c. Cost-plus pricing
d. Price discrimination

25. _____ in economics and business is the result of an exchange and from that trade we assign a numerical monetary value to a good, service or asset. If Alice trades Bob 4 apples for an orange, the _____ of an orange is 4 apples. Inversely, the _____ of an apple is 1/4 oranges.

a. Discounts and allowances
b. Price
c. Transactional Net Margin Method
d. Price discrimination

26. _____ is a pricing technique applied to public goods, which is a particular case of a Lindahl equilibrium. Instead of different demands for the same public good, we consider the demands for a public good in different periods of the day, month or year, then finding the optimal capacity (quantity supplied) and, afterwards, the optimal peak-load prices.

This has particular applications in public goods such as public urban transportation, where day demand (peak period) is usually much higher than night demand (off-peak period).

a. 3M Company
b. Peak-load pricing
c. BMC Software, Inc.
d. BNSF Railway

27. _____ exists when sales of identical goods or services are transacted at different prices from the same provider. In a theoretical market with perfect information, no transaction costs or prohibition on secondary exchange (or re-selling) to prevent arbitrage, _____ can only be a feature of monopoly and oligopoly markets, where market power can be exercised. Otherwise, the moment the seller tries to sell the same good at different prices, the buyer at the lower price can arbitrage by selling to the consumer buying at the higher price but with a tiny discount.

a. Resale price maintenance
b. Transactional Net Margin Method
c. Price
d. Price discrimination

28. _____, known in the United States as antitrust law, has three main elements:

- prohibiting agreements or practices that restrict free trading and competition between business entities. This includes in particular the repression of cartels.
- banning abusive behaviour by a firm dominating a market, or anti-competitive practices that tend to lead to such a dominant position. Practices controlled in this way may include predatory pricing, tying, price gouging, refusal to deal, and many others.
- supervising the mergers and acquisitions of large corporations, including some joint ventures. Transactions that are considered to threaten the competitive process can be prohibited altogether, or approved subject to 'remedies' such as an obligation to divest part of the merged business or to offer licences or access to facilities to enable other businesses to continue competing.

The substance and practice of _____ varies from jurisdiction to jurisdiction. Protecting the interests of consumers (consumer welfare) and ensuring that entrepreneurs have an opportunity to compete in the market economy are often treated as important objectives. _____ is closely connected with law on deregulation of access to markets, state aids and subsidies, the privatisation of state owned assets and the establishment of independent sector regulators. In recent decades, _____ has been viewed as a way to provide better public services.

a. Hospital Survey and Construction Act
b. Lease
c. Malpractice
d. Competition law

29. The _____ is an independent agency of the United States government, established in 1914 by the _____ Act. Its principal mission is the promotion of 'consumer protection' and the elimination and prevention of what regulators perceive to be harmfully 'anti-competitive' business practices, such as coercive monopoly.

The _____ Act was one of President Wilson's major acts against trusts.

a. BMC Software, Inc.
b. 3M Company
c. BNSF Railway
d. Federal Trade Commission

30. _____ is the practice of selling a product or service at a very low price, intending to drive competitors out of the market, or create barriers to entry for potential new competitors. If competitors or potential competitors cannot sustain equal or lower prices without losing money, they go out of business or choose not to enter the business. The predatory merchant then has fewer competitors or is even a de facto monopoly, and can then raise prices above what the market would otherwise bear.

a. 3M Company
b. BNSF Railway
c. BMC Software, Inc.
d. Predatory pricing

31. The _____ of 1936 (or Anti-Price Discrimination Act, 15 U.S.C. § 13) is a United States federal law that prohibits what were considered, at the time of passage, to be anticompetitive practices by producers, specifically price discrimination. It grew out of practices in which chain stores were allowed to purchase goods at lower prices than other retailers.
a. Limited liability
b. Consumer protection laws
c. Lien
d. Robinson-Patman Act

Chapter 13. Strategy, Balanced Scorecard, and Strategic Profitability Analysis

1. In economics, business, retail, and accounting, a _____ is the value of money that has been used up to produce something, and hence is not available for use anymore. In economics, a _____ is an alternative that is given up as a result of a decision. In business, the _____ may be one of acquisition, in which case the amount of money expended to acquire it is counted as _____.
   a. Cost of quality
   b. Cost allocation
   c. Cost
   d. Prime cost

2. _____ is a concept developed by Michael Porter, used in business strategy. It describes a way to establish the competitive advantage. _____, in basic words, means the lowest cost of operation in the industry.
   a. Strategic business unit
   b. BMC Software, Inc.
   c. 3M Company
   d. Cost leadership

3. In marketing, _____ is the process of distinguishing the differences of a product or offering from others, to make it more attractive to a particular target market. This involves differentiating it from competitors' products as well as one's own product offerings.
   a. Value chain
   b. Market segmentation
   c. Market segment
   d. Product differentiation

4. _____ is the realization of an application idea, model, design, specification, standard, algorithm an _____ is a realization of a technical specification or algorithm as a program, software component, or other computer system. Many _____s may exist for a given specification or standard.
   a. AMEX
   b. AIG
   c. ABC Television Network
   d. Implementation

5. A _____, also client, buyer or purchaser is the buyer or user of the paid products of an individual or organization, mostly called the supplier or seller. This is typically through purchasing or renting goods or services.

Chapter 13. Strategy, Balanced Scorecard, and Strategic Profitability Analysis

a. BMC Software, Inc.
b. BNSF Railway
c. 3M Company
d. Customer

6. In economics, _____ or _____ goods or real _____ refers to factors of production used to create goods or services that are not themselves significantly consumed (though they may depreciate) in the production process. _____ goods may be acquired with money or financial _____. In finance and accounting, _____ generally refers to financial wealth, especially that used to start or maintain a business.

a. Disclosure
b. Screening
c. Vyborg Appeal
d. Capital

7. _____ is the planning process used to determine whether a firm's long term investments such as new machinery, replacement machinery, new plants, new products, and research development projects are worth pursuing. It is budget for major capital, or investment, expenditures.

Many formal methods are used in _____, including the techniques such as

- Net present value
- Profitability index
- Internal rate of return
- Modified Internal Rate of Return
- Equivalent annuity

These methods use the incremental cash flows from each potential investment, or project. Techniques based on accounting earnings and accounting rules are sometimes used - though economists consider this to be improper - such as the accounting rate of return, and 'return on investment.' Simplified and hybrid methods are used as well, such as payback period and discounted payback period.

a. Gross profit
b. Preferred stock
c. Cash flow
d. Capital budgeting

8. The _____ is a performance management tool which began as a concept for measuring whether the smaller-scale operational activities of a company are aligned with its larger-scale objectives in terms of vision and strategy.

By focusing not only on financial outcomes but also on the operational, marketing and developmental inputs to these, the _____ helps provide a more comprehensive view of a business, which in turn helps organizations act in their best long-term interests. This tool is also being used to address business response to climate change and greenhouse gas emissions.

a. Best practice
b. Trustee
c. Management by objectives
d. Balanced scorecard

9. _____ is the difference between operating revenues and operating expenses, but it is also sometimes used as a synonym for EBIT and operating profit. This is true if the firm has no non-_____.

A professional investor contemplating a change to the capital structure of a firm first evaluates a firm's fundamental earnings potential (reflected by Earnings Before Interest, Taxes, Depreciation and Amortization EBITDA and EBIT), and then determines the optimal use of debt vs. equity.

a. AMEX
b. ABC Television Network
c. AIG
d. Operating income

10. _____ in economics refers to metrics and measures of output from production processes, per unit of input. Labor _____, for example, is typically measured as a ratio of output per labor-hour, an input. _____ may be conceived of as a metrics of the technical or engineering efficiency of production.
a. Value engineering
b. Productivity
c. Deming Prize
d. Cellular manufacturing

11. In business, _____, Overhead cost or _____ expense refers to an ongoing expense of operating a business. The term _____ is usually used to group expenses that are necessary to the continued functioning of the business, but do not directly generate profits.

_____ expenses are all costs on the income statement except for direct labor and direct materials.

Chapter 13. Strategy, Balanced Scorecard, and Strategic Profitability Analysis

a. AIG
b. ABC Television Network
c. Intangible assets
d. Overhead

12. In economics, _____ is a variable which accounts for effects in total output not caused by inputs. For example, a year with unusually good weather will tend to have higher output, because bad weather hinders agricultural output. A variable like weather does not directly relate to unit inputs, so weather is considered a _____ variable.
    a. Joseph Ronald Banister
    b. Maturity
    c. Total-factor productivity
    d. Screening

13. In mathematics _____s are numbers or other things that get multiplied. In particular, see:

- Factorization, the decomposition of an object into a product of other objects
- Integer factorization, the process of breaking down a composite number into smaller non-trivial divisors
- A coefficient
- A divisor of a particular number, or of an element of a monoid
- A von Neumann algebra with a trivial center

In statistics

- _____ analysis is the study of how _____s or certain variables affect variables.

In technology:

- Human _____s, a profession that focuses on how people interact with products, tools, or procedures
- 'Functionality, Application domain, Conditions, Technology, Objects and Responsibility;', In object-oriented programming

In computer science and information technology:

- Authentication _____, a piece of information used to verify a person's identity for security purposes
- _____, a Unix command for numbers factorization
- _____ (programming language), an experimental Forth-like programming language

80 *Chapter 13. Strategy, Balanced Scorecard, and Strategic Profitability Analysis*

In television:

- The O'Reilly _____, an American talk show hosted by Bill O'Reilly on Fox News.
- The Krypton _____, a British game show hosted by Gordon Burns, formally on ITV. Also had an American version.

a. Merck ' Co., Inc.
b. Factor
c. Valuation
d. The Goodyear Tire ' Rubber Company

Chapter 14. Cost Allocation, Customer-Profitability Analysis, and Sales-Variance
Analysis

1. In economics, business, retail, and accounting, a _____ is the value of money that has been used up to produce something, and hence is not available for use anymore. In economics, a _____ is an alternative that is given up as a result of a decision. In business, the _____ may be one of acquisition, in which case the amount of money expended to acquire it is counted as _____.
    a. Prime cost
    b. Cost allocation
    c. Cost of quality
    d. Cost

2. _____ is a process of attributing cost to particular cost centres. For example the wage of the driver of the purchasing department can be allocated to the purchasing department cost centre. It is not necessary to share the wage cost over several different cost centers.
    a. Variable cost
    b. Cost of quality
    c. Cost accounting
    d. Cost allocation

3. Homogeneity means 'being similar throughout'.

Homogeneity may also refer to:

- _____, a variety of meanings
- In statistics homogeneity can refer to
    o Homogeneity of variance: Homoscedasticity
    o Logically consistent data matrices: homogeneity (statistics)
- Homogeneity (physics), in physics, two particular meanings: On one hand, translational invariance. On the other, homogeneity of units in equations, related to dimensional analysis
- Homogenetic or homoplastic, in biology, applied both to animals and plants, of having a resemblance in structure, due to descent from a common progenitor with subsequent modification
- Homogenization is intensive mixing of mutually insoluble phases (sometimes with addition of surfactants) to obtain a soluble suspension or emulsion, for example homogenizing milk so that the cream doesn't separate out
- In physical chemistry, _____ describes a single-phase system as opposed to a heterogeneous system. See also phase diagrams and the classification of catalysts
- In the context of procurement/purchasing, _____ is used to describe goods that do not vary in their essential characteristic irrespective of the source of supply

Chapter 14. Cost Allocation, Customer-Profitability Analysis, and Sales-Variance Analysis

a. Procter ' Gamble
b. Homogeneous
c. Scientific Research and Experimental Development Tax Incentive Program
d. Serial bonds

4. A _____, also client, buyer or purchaser is the buyer or user of the paid products of an individual or organization, mostly called the supplier or seller. This is typically through purchasing or renting goods or services.
a. BNSF Railway
b. 3M Company
c. Customer
d. BMC Software, Inc.

5. _____ in economics and business is the result of an exchange and from that trade we assign a numerical monetary value to a good, service or asset. If Alice trades Bob 4 apples for an orange, the _____ of an orange is 4 apples. Inversely, the _____ of an apple is 1/4 oranges.
a. Transactional Net Margin Method
b. Price
c. Discounts and allowances
d. Price discrimination

6. _____ is a financial mechanism in which a debtor obtains the right to delay payments to a creditor, for a defined period of time, in exchange for a charge or fee. Essentially, the party that owes money in the present purchases the right to delay the payment until some future date. The discount, or charge, is simply the difference between the original amount owed in the present and the amount that has to be paid in the future to settle the debt.
a. Discounting
b. Risk aversion
c. Discount factor
d. Risk adjusted return on capital

7. A _____ is the pinnacle activity involved in selling products or services in return for money or other compensation. It is an act of completion of a commercial activity.

A _____ is completed by the seller, the owner of the goods.

Chapter 14. Cost Allocation, Customer-Profitability Analysis, and Sales-Variance Analysis

a. Tertiary sector of economy
b. Maturity
c. High yield stock
d. Sale

8. In probability theory and statistics, the _____ of a random variable, probability distribution averaging the squared distance of its possible values from the expected value (mean.) Whereas the mean is a way to describe the location of a distribution, the _____ is a way to capture its scale or degree of being spread out. The unit of _____ is the square of the unit of the original variable.
    a. Variance
    b. Monte Carlo methods
    c. Statistics
    d. Time series

9. In finance, the term _____ describes the amount in cash that returns to the owners of a security. Normally it does not include the price variations, at the difference of the total return. _____ applies to various stated rates of return on stocks (common and preferred, and convertible), fixed income instruments (bonds, notes, bills, strips, zero coupon), and some other investment type insurance products (e.g. annuities.)
    a. Pension System
    b. Disclosure
    c. Yield
    d. Residence trusts

Chapter 15. Allocation of Support-Department Costs, Common Costs and Revenues

1. In economics, business, retail, and accounting, a _____ is the value of money that has been used up to produce something, and hence is not available for use anymore. In economics, a _____ is an alternative that is given up as a result of a decision. In business, the _____ may be one of acquisition, in which case the amount of money expended to acquire it is counted as _____.
   a. Cost of quality
   b. Cost allocation
   c. Prime cost
   d. Cost

2. _____ is a process of attributing cost to particular cost centres. For example the wage of the driver of the purchasing department can be allocated to the purchasing department cost centre. It is not necessary to share the wage cost over several different cost centers.
   a. Cost accounting
   b. Cost of quality
   c. Variable cost
   d. Cost allocation

3. An _____ is the buying of one company by another. An _____ may be friendly or hostile. In the former case, the companies cooperate in negotiations; in the latter case, the takeover target is unwilling to be bought or the target's board has no prior knowledge of the offer. _____ usually refers to a purchase of a smaller firm by a larger one. Sometimes, however, a smaller firm will acquire management control of a larger or longer established company and keep its name for the combined entity. This is known as a reverse takeover.
   a. AMEX
   b. AIG
   c. ABC Television Network
   d. Acquisition

4. In management accounting, _____ establishes budget and actual cost of operations, processes, departments or product and the analysis of variances, profitability or social use of funds. Managers use _____ to support decision-making to cut a company's costs and improve profitability. As a form of management accounting, _____ need not follow standards such as GAAP, because its primary use is for internal managers, rather than outside users, and what to compute is instead decided pragmatically.
   a. Cost Accounting
   b. Prime cost
   c. Cost-volume-profit analysis
   d. Marginal cost

5. A _____ is a permanent or semi-permanent organization in the machinery of government that is responsible for the oversight and administration of specific functions, such as an intelligence agency. There is a notable variety of types of agency. Although usage differs, a _____ is normally distinct both from a Department or Ministry, and other types of public body established by government.
   a. BMC Software, Inc.
   b. 3M Company
   c. BNSF Railway
   d. Government agency

6. A _____ is the pinnacle activity involved in selling products or services in return for money or other compensation. It is an act of completion of a commercial activity.

A _____ is completed by the seller, the owner of the goods.

   a. High yield stock
   b. Maturity
   c. Sale
   d. Tertiary sector of economy

7. _____ are costs that are not directly accountable to a particular function or product. _____ may be either fixed or variable. _____ include taxes, administration, personnel and security costs, and are also known as overhead.
   a. ABC Television Network
   b. Activity-based management
   c. Activity-based costing
   d. Indirect costs

Chapter 16. Cost Allocation: Joint Products and Byproducts

1. In economics, business, retail, and accounting, a _____ is the value of money that has been used up to produce something, and hence is not available for use anymore. In economics, a _____ is an alternative that is given up as a result of a decision. In business, the _____ may be one of acquisition, in which case the amount of money expended to acquire it is counted as _____.
   a. Cost allocation
   b. Cost of quality
   c. Cost
   d. Prime cost

2. A _____ is the pinnacle activity involved in selling products or services in return for money or other compensation. It is an act of completion of a commercial activity.

   A _____ is completed by the seller, the owner of the goods.

   a. Tertiary sector of economy
   b. Maturity
   c. Sale
   d. High yield stock

3. _____ is a method of evaluating an asset's worth when held in inventory, in the field of accounting. _____ is part of the Generally Accepted Accounting Principles that apply to valuing inventory, so as to not overstate or understate the value of inventory goods. Net realisable value is generally equal to the selling price of the inventory goods less the selling costs (completion and disposal).
   a. BMC Software, Inc.
   b. Revenue recognition
   c. 3M Company
   d. Net realizable value

4. _____ can be regarded as an outcome of mental processes (cognitive process) leading to the selection of a course of action among several alternatives. Every _____ process produces a final choice. The output can be an action or an opinion of choice.
   a. 3M Company
   b. BMC Software, Inc.
   c. BNSF Railway
   d. Decision making

5. _____, in managerial economics is a form of cost accounting. It is a simplified model, useful for elementary instruction and for short-run decisions.

Chapter 16. Cost Allocation: Joint Products and Byproducts

Cost-volume-profit (CVP) analysis expands the use of information provided by breakeven analysis.

a. Cost of quality
b. Fixed costs
c. Cost-volume-profit analysis
d. Cost accounting

6. _____ is systematic determination of merit, worth, and significance of something or someone using criteria against a set of standards. _____ often is used to characterize and appraise subjects of interest in a wide range of human enterprises, including the arts, criminal justice, foundations and non-profit organizations, government, health care, and other human services.

Depending on the topic of interest, there are professional groups which look to the quality and rigor of the _____ process.

a. AIG
b. ABC Television Network
c. AMEX
d. Evaluation

Chapter 17. Process Costing

1. _____ is an accounting methodology that traces and accumulates direct costs, and allocates indirect costs of a manufacturing process. Costs are assigned to products, usually in a large batch, which might include an entire month's production. Eventually, costs have to be allocated to individual units of product.
   a. Cost driver
   b. Cost management
   c. Process costing
   d. Profit center

Chapter 18. Spoilage, Rework, and Scrap

1. _____ is an accounting methodology that traces and accumulates direct costs, and allocates indirect costs of a manufacturing process. Costs are assigned to products, usually in a large batch, which might include an entire month's production. Eventually, costs have to be allocated to individual units of product.
   a. Cost management
   b. Cost driver
   c. Profit center
   d. Process Costing

2. A _____ has several related meanings:

   - a daily record of events or business; a private _____ is usually referred to as a diary.
   - a newspaper or other periodical, in the literal sense of one published each day;
   - many publications issued at stated intervals, such as magazines, or scholarly academic _____s, or the record of the transactions of a society, are often called _____s. Although _____ is sometimes used, erroneously, as a synonym for 'magazine,' in academic use, a _____ refers to a serious, scholarly publication, most often peer-reviewed. A non-scholarly magazine written for an educated audience about an industry or an area of professional activity is usually called a professional magazine.

   The word 'journalist' for one whose business is writing for the public press has been in use since the end of the 17th century.

   Open access _____s are scholarly _____s that are available to the reader without financial or other barrier other than access to the internet itself. Some are subsidized, and some require payment on behalf of the author. Subsidized _____s are financed by an academic institution or a government information center.

   a. 3M Company
   b. Journal
   c. BNSF Railway
   d. BMC Software, Inc.

3. In economics, business, retail, and accounting, a _____ is the value of money that has been used up to produce something, and hence is not available for use anymore. In economics, a _____ is an alternative that is given up as a result of a decision. In business, the _____ may be one of acquisition, in which case the amount of money expended to acquire it is counted as _____.
   a. Prime cost
   b. Cost allocation
   c. Cost of quality
   d. Cost

4. A _____ is the pinnacle activity involved in selling products or services in return for money or other compensation. It is an act of completion of a commercial activity.

A _____ is completed by the seller, the owner of the goods.

a. Tertiary sector of economy
b. High yield stock
c. Maturity
d. Sale

5. _____ is the difference between operating revenues and operating expenses, but it is also sometimes used as a synonym for EBIT and operating profit. This is true if the firm has no non-_____.

A professional investor contemplating a change to the capital structure of a firm first evaluates a firm's fundamental earnings potential (reflected by Earnings Before Interest, Taxes, Depreciation and Amortization EBITDA and EBIT), and then determines the optimal use of debt vs. equity.

a. AMEX
b. AIG
c. ABC Television Network
d. Operating income

Chapter 19. Balanced Scorecard: Quality, Time, and the Theory of Constraints

1. The _____ is a performance management tool which began as a concept for measuring whether the smaller-scale operational activities of a company are aligned with its larger-scale objectives in terms of vision and strategy.

By focusing not only on financial outcomes but also on the operational, marketing and developmental inputs to these, the _____ helps provide a more comprehensive view of a business, which in turn helps organizations act in their best long-term interests. This tool is also being used to address business response to climate change and greenhouse gas emissions.

   a. Trustee
   b. Best practice
   c. Management by objectives
   d. Balanced scorecard

2. American Society for Quality (ASQ), formerly known as _____, is a knowledge-based global community of quality control experts, with nearly 85,000 members dedicated to the promotion and advancement of quality tools, principles, and practices in their workplaces and in their communities.

Established in 1946 and based in Milwaukee, ASQ traces its beginnings to the end of World War II, as quality experts and manufacturers sought ways to sustain the many quality-improvement techniques used during wartime. ASQ has played an important role in upholding these standards from the past while championing continued innovation in the field of quality.

   a. AIG
   b. International Monetary Fund
   c. American Society for Quality Control
   d. ABC Television Network

3. The _____, established in December 1950 in honor of W. Edwards Deming, was originally designed to reward Japanese companies for major advances in quality improvement. Over the years it has grown, under the guidance of Japanese Union of Scientists and Engineers (JUSE) to where it is now also available to non-Japanese companies, albeit usually operating in Japan, and also to individuals recognized as having made major contributions to the advancement of quality. The awards ceremony is broadcast every year in Japan on national television.
   a. Changeover
   b. Productivity
   c. Value engineering
   d. Deming Prize

4. The _____, widely known as ISO , is an international-standard-setting body composed of representatives from various national standards organizations. Founded on 23 February 1947, the organization promulgates worldwide proprietary industrial and commercial standards. It is headquartered in Geneva, Switzerland.

Chapter 19. Balanced Scorecard: Quality, Time, and the Theory of Constraints

a. AMEX
b. AIG
c. ABC Television Network
d. International Organization for Standardization

5. In engineering and manufacturing, _____ and quality engineering are used in developing systems to ensure products or services are designed and produced to meet or exceed customer requirements. Refer to the definition by Merriam-Webster for further information . These systems are often developed in conjunction with other business and engineering disciplines using a cross-functional approach.
   a. BMC Software, Inc.
   b. BNSF Railway
   c. 3M Company
   d. Quality Control

6. In economics, business, retail, and accounting, a _____ is the value of money that has been used up to produce something, and hence is not available for use anymore. In economics, a _____ is an alternative that is given up as a result of a decision. In business, the _____ may be one of acquisition, in which case the amount of money expended to acquire it is counted as _____.
   a. Cost
   b. Cost allocation
   c. Prime cost
   d. Cost of quality

7. The concept of _____ is a means to quantify the total cost of quality-related efforts and deficiencies. It was first described by Armand V. Feigenbaum in a 1956 Harvard Business Review article.

Prior to its introduction, the general perception was that higher quality requires higher costs, either by buying better materials or machines or by hiring more labor.

   a. Cost allocation
   b. Marginal cost
   c. Variable cost
   d. Quality costs

Chapter 19. Balanced Scorecard: Quality, Time, and the Theory of Constraints

8. An _____ is a term used in behavioral economics to describe those types of behaviors that impose costs on a person in the long-run that are not taken into account when making decisions in the present. Classical Economics discourages government from creating legislation that targets internalities, because it is assumed that the consumer takes these personal costs into account when paying for the good that causes the _____. For example, cigarettes should be taxed because of the negative consumption externalities that they impose, such as second-hand smoke, not because the smoker harms him or herself by smoking.
   a. Internality
   b. Inventory turnover ratio
   c. Operating budget
   d. Authorised capital

9. A _____, also client, buyer or purchaser is the buyer or user of the paid products of an individual or organization, mostly called the supplier or seller. This is typically through purchasing or renting goods or services.
   a. BMC Software, Inc.
   b. Customer
   c. BNSF Railway
   d. 3M Company

10. In economics, _____ or _____ goods or real _____ refers to factors of production used to create goods or services that are not themselves significantly consumed (though they may depreciate) in the production process. _____ goods may be acquired with money or financial _____. In finance and accounting, _____ generally refers to financial wealth, especially that used to start or maintain a business.
    a. Vyborg Appeal
    b. Disclosure
    c. Screening
    d. Capital

11. _____ is the planning process used to determine whether a firm's long term investments such as new machinery, replacement machinery, new plants, new products, and research development projects are worth pursuing. It is budget for major capital, or investment, expenditures.

Many formal methods are used in _____, including the techniques such as

- Net present value
- Profitability index
- Internal rate of return
- Modified Internal Rate of Return
- Equivalent annuity

These methods use the incremental cash flows from each potential investment, or project. Techniques based on accounting earnings and accounting rules are sometimes used - though economists consider this to be improper - such as the accounting rate of return, and 'return on investment.' Simplified and hybrid methods are used as well, such as payback period and discounted payback period.

a. Gross profit
b. Preferred stock
c. Cash flow
d. Capital budgeting

12. _____, a business term, is a measure of how products and services supplied by a company meet or surpass customer expectation. It is seen as a key performance indicator within business and is part of the four perspectives of a Balanced Scorecard.

In a competitive marketplace where businesses compete for customers, _____ is seen as a key differentiator and increasingly has become a key element of business strategy.

a. Time to market
b. Procurement
c. Customer satisfaction
d. Pre-determined overhead rate

13. In mathematics and statistics, the _____ of a list of numbers is the sum of all of the list divided by the number of items in the list. If the list is a statistical population, then the mean of that population is called a population mean. If the list is a statistical sample, we call the resulting statistic a sample mean.

a. AMEX
b. ABC Television Network
c. AIG
d. Arithmetic mean

14. In probability theory and statistics, _____ is a measure of the variability or dispersion of a population, a data set, or a probability distribution. A low _____ indicates that the data points tend to be very close to the same value (the mean), while high _____ indicates that the data are 'spread out' over a large range of values.

For example, the average height for adult men in the United States is about 70 inches, with a _____ of around 3 inches.

a. Probability distribution
b. Moving average
c. Standard deviation
d. Variance

15. _____ is an effective method of monitoring a process through the use of control charts. Control charts enable the use of objective criteria for distinguishing background variation from events of significance based on statistical techniques. Much of its power lies in the ability to monitor both process center and its variation about that center.
    a. BMC Software, Inc.
    b. BNSF Railway
    c. 3M Company
    d. Statistical process control

16. In probability theory and statistics, the _____ (or expectation value or mean and for continuous random variables with a density function it is the probability density-weighted integral of the possible values.

The term '_____' can be misleading.

    a. ABC Television Network
    b. AMEX
    c. Expected value
    d. AIG

17. Employment is a contract between two parties, one being the employer and the other being the _____. An _____ may be defined as: 'A person in the service of another under any contract of hire, express or implied, oral or written, where the employer has the power or right to control and direct the _____ in the material details of how the work is to be performed.' Black's Law Dictionary page 471 (5th ed. 1979.)
    a. AMEX
    b. ABC Television Network
    c. Employee
    d. AIG

18. _____ refers to increasing the spiritual, political, social or economic strength of individuals and communities. It often involves the empowered developing confidence in their own capacities.

The term Human _____ covers a vast landscape of meanings, interpretations, definitions and disciplines ranging from psychology and philosophy to the highly commercialized Self-Help industry and Motivational sciences.

a. Entity
b. IMF
c. IPO
d. Empowerment

19. _____ is systematic determination of merit, worth, and significance of something or someone using criteria against a set of standards. _____ often is used to characterize and appraise subjects of interest in a wide range of human enterprises, including the arts, criminal justice, foundations and non-profit organizations, government, health care, and other human services.

Depending on the topic of interest, there are professional groups which look to the quality and rigor of the _____ process.

a. AMEX
b. AIG
c. ABC Television Network
d. Evaluation

20. A _____ is the period of time between the initiation of any process of production and the completion of that process. Thus the _____ for ordering a new car from a manufacturer may be anywhere from 2 weeks to 6 months. In industry, _____ reduction is an important part of lean manufacturing.

a. BMC Software, Inc.
b. 3M Company
c. Lead time
d. BNSF Railway

21. _____ is a term used in subtly different ways in a number of fields, including philosophy, physics, statistics, economics, finance, insurance, psychology, sociology, engineering, and information science. It applies to predictions of future events, to physical measurements already made, or to the unknown.

In his seminal work Risk, _____, and Profit University of Chicago economist Frank Knight (1921) established the important distinction between risk and _____:

'_____ must be taken in a sense radically distinct from the familiar notion of risk, from which it has never been properly separated....

a. Uncertainty
b. ABC Television Network
c. AMEX
d. AIG

22. _____ is an overall management philosophy introduced by Dr. Eliyahu M. Goldratt in his 1984 book titled The Goal, that is geared to help organizations continually achieve their goal. The title comes from the contention that any manageable system is limited in achieving more of its goal by a very small number of constraints, and that there is always at least one constraint. The _____ process seeks to identify the constraint and restructure the rest of the organization around it, through the use of the Five Focusing Steps.
   a. Theory of constraints
   b. Six Sigma
   c. Lean production
   d. Lean manufacturing

23. _____ is a costing model that identifies activities in an organization and assigns the cost of each activity resource to all products and services according to the actual consumption by each: it assigns more indirect costs (overhead) into direct costs.

In this way an organization can establish the true cost of its individual products and services for the purposes of identifying and eliminating those which are unprofitable and lowering the prices of those which are overpriced.

In a business organization, the ABC methodology assigns an organization's resource costs through activities to the products and services provided to its customers.

   a. ABC Television Network
   b. Indirect costs
   c. Activity-based costing
   d. Activity-based management

Chapter 20. Inventory Management, Just-in-Time, and Backflush Costing

1. _____ consists of the sale of goods or merchandise from a fixed location, such as a department store, boutique or kiosk in small or individual lots for direct consumption by the purchaser. _____ may include subordinated services, such as delivery. Purchasers may be individuals or businesses.
   a. Retailing
   b. 3M Company
   c. BNSF Railway
   d. BMC Software, Inc.

2. Just in Time could refer to the following:

   • _____, an inventory strategy that reduces in-process inventory
   • _____ compilation, a technique for improving the performance of bytecode-compiled programming systems

   a. Comparable
   b. Help desk and incident reporting auditing
   c. Just-in-time
   d. Fiscal

3. In economics, business, retail, and accounting, a _____ is the value of money that has been used up to produce something, and hence is not available for use anymore. In economics, a _____ is an alternative that is given up as a result of a decision. In business, the _____ may be one of acquisition, in which case the amount of money expended to acquire it is counted as _____.
   a. Prime cost
   b. Cost
   c. Cost allocation
   d. Cost of quality

4. _____ refers to a business or organization attempting to acquire goods or services to accomplish the goals of the enterprise. Though there are several organizations that attempt to set standards in the _____ process, processes can vary greatly between organizations. Typically the word e;_____e; is not used interchangeably with the word e;procuremente;, since procurement typically includes Expediting, Supplier Quality, and Traffic and Logistics (T'L) in addition to _____.
   a. Supply chain
   b. Consignor
   c. Free port
   d. Purchasing

Chapter 20. Inventory Management, Just-in-Time, and Backflush Costing 99

5. The concept of _____ is a means to quantify the total cost of quality-related efforts and deficiencies. It was first described by Armand V. Feigenbaum in a 1956 Harvard Business Review article.

Prior to its introduction, the general perception was that higher quality requires higher costs, either by buying better materials or machines or by hiring more labor.

   a. Variable cost
   b. Cost allocation
   c. Quality costs
   d. Marginal cost

6. A _____ is the pinnacle activity involved in selling products or services in return for money or other compensation. It is an act of completion of a commercial activity.

A _____ is completed by the seller, the owner of the goods.

   a. Tertiary sector of economy
   b. Sale
   c. Maturity
   d. High yield stock

7. A _____ is the period of time between the initiation of any process of production and the completion of that process. Thus the _____ for ordering a new car from a manufacturer may be anywhere from 2 weeks to 6 months. In industry, _____ reduction is an important part of lean manufacturing.
   a. BNSF Railway
   b. Lead time
   c. 3M Company
   d. BMC Software, Inc.

8. The _____ is the level of inventory when a fresh order should be made with suppliers to bring the inventory up by the Economic order quantity ('EOQ'.)

The _____ for replenishment of stock occurs when the level of inventory drops down to zero. In view of instantaneous replenishment of stock the level of inventory jumps to the original level from zero level.

a. 3M Company
b. FIFO and LIFO accounting
c. Finished good
d. Reorder point

9. _____ is a term used by inventory specialists to describe a level of extra stock that is maintained below the cycle stock to buffer against stockouts. _____ exists to counter uncertainties in supply and demand. _____ is defined as extra units of inventory carried as protection against possible stockouts .(shortfall in raw material or packaging.)
a. Proprietorship
b. Tax profit
c. Sensitivity analysis
d. Safety stock

10. _____ is systematic determination of merit, worth, and significance of something or someone using criteria against a set of standards. _____ often is used to characterize and appraise subjects of interest in a wide range of human enterprises, including the arts, criminal justice, foundations and non-profit organizations, government, health care, and other human services.

Depending on the topic of interest, there are professional groups which look to the quality and rigor of the _____ process.

a. AIG
b. ABC Television Network
c. AMEX
d. Evaluation

11. A '_____ is the system of organizations, people, technology, activities, information and resources involved in moving a product or service from supplier to customer. _____ activities transform natural resources, raw materials and components into a finished product that is delivered to the end customer. In sophisticated _____ systems, used products may re-enter the _____ at any point where residual value is recyclable.
a. Purchasing
b. Consignor
c. Free port
d. Supply chain

Chapter 20. Inventory Management, Just-in-Time, and Backflush Costing

12. _____ is a family of business models in which the buyer of a product provides certain information to a supplier of that product and the supplier takes full responsibility for maintaining an agreed inventory of the material, usually at the buyer's consumption location (usually a store.) A third party logistics provider can also be involved to make sure that the buyer have the required level of inventory by adjusting the demand and supply gaps.

As a symbiotic relationship, _____ makes it less likely that a business will unintentionally become out of stock of a good and reduces inventory in the supply chain.

   a. BNSF Railway
   b. 3M Company
   c. BMC Software, Inc.
   d. Vendor Managed Inventory

13. Lean manufacturing or _____, which is often known simply as 'Lean', is a production practice that considers the expenditure of resources for any goal other than the creation of value for the end customer to be wasteful, and thus a target for elimination. Working from the perspective of the customer who consumes a product or service, 'value' is defined as any action or process that a customer would be willing to pay for. Basically, lean is centered around creating more value with less work.
   a. Lean manufacturing
   b. Make to order
   c. Six Sigma
   d. Lean production

14. _____ is a company-wide computer software system used to manage and coordinate all the resources, information, and functions of a business from shared data stores.

An _____ system has a service-oriented architecture with modular hardware and software units or 'services' that communicate on a local area network. The modular design allows a business to add or reconfigure modules (perhaps from different vendors) while preserving data integrity in one shared database that may be centralized or distributed.

   a. ABC Television Network
   b. AIG
   c. AMEX
   d. Enterprise Resource Planning

15. An _____ allows a company to provide a monetary value for items that make up their inventory. Inventories are usually the largest current asset of a business, and proper measurement of them is necessary to assure accurate financial statements. If inventory is not properly measured, expenses and revenues cannot be properly matched and a company could make poor business decisions.

a. Inventory valuation
b. ABC Television Network
c. AMEX
d. AIG

16. _____ is the realization of an application idea, model, design, specification, standard, algorithm an _____ is a realization of a technical specification or algorithm as a program, software component, or other computer system. Many _____s may exist for a given specification or standard.
a. ABC Television Network
b. AMEX
c. AIG
d. Implementation

17. In finance, _____ is the process of estimating the potential market value of a financial asset or liability. They can be done on assets (for example, investments in marketable securities such as stocks, options, business enterprises, or intangible assets such as patents and trademarks) or on liabilities (e.g., Bonds issued by a company.) A _____ is required in many contexts including investment analysis, capital budgeting, merger and acquisition transactions, financial reporting, taxable events to determine the proper tax liability, and in litigation.
a. Valuation
b. Vyborg Appeal
c. Disclosure
d. Daybook

18. In probability theory and statistics, the _____ of a random variable, probability distribution averaging the squared distance of its possible values from the expected value (mean.) Whereas the mean is a way to describe the location of a distribution, the _____ is a way to capture its scale or degree of being spread out. The unit of _____ is the square of the unit of the original variable.
a. Time series
b. Monte Carlo methods
c. Statistics
d. Variance

19. _____ is a costing model that identifies activities in an organization and assigns the cost of each activity resource to all products and services according to the actual consumption by each: it assigns more indirect costs (overhead) into direct costs.

In this way an organization can establish the true cost of its individual products and services for the purposes of identifying and eliminating those which are unprofitable and lowering the prices of those which are overpriced.

In a business organization, the ABC methodology assigns an organization's resource costs through activities to the products and services provided to its customers.

a. Activity-based management
b. ABC Television Network
c. Indirect costs
d. Activity-based costing

20. _____ is the term used to refer to the standard framework of guidelines for financial accounting used in any given jurisdiction. _____ includes the standards, conventions, and rules accountants follow in recording and summarizing transactions, and in the preparation of financial statements.

Financial accounting information must be assembled and reported objectively.

a. General ledger
b. Generally accepted accounting principles
c. Current asset
d. Long-term liabilities

1. In economics, business, retail, and accounting, a _____ is the value of money that has been used up to produce something, and hence is not available for use anymore. In economics, a _____ is an alternative that is given up as a result of a decision. In business, the _____ may be one of acquisition, in which case the amount of money expended to acquire it is counted as _____.
   a. Cost of quality
   b. Cost allocation
   c. Prime cost
   d. Cost

2. In economics, _____ or _____ goods or real _____ refers to factors of production used to create goods or services that are not themselves significantly consumed (though they may depreciate) in the production process. _____ goods may be acquired with money or financial _____. In finance and accounting, _____ generally refers to financial wealth, especially that used to start or maintain a business.
   a. Disclosure
   b. Vyborg Appeal
   c. Screening
   d. Capital

3. _____ is the planning process used to determine whether a firm's long term investments such as new machinery, replacement machinery, new plants, new products, and research development projects are worth pursuing. It is budget for major capital, or investment, expenditures.

Many formal methods are used in _____, including the techniques such as

- Net present value
- Profitability index
- Internal rate of return
- Modified Internal Rate of Return
- Equivalent annuity

These methods use the incremental cash flows from each potential investment, or project. Techniques based on accounting earnings and accounting rules are sometimes used - though economists consider this to be improper - such as the accounting rate of return, and 'return on investment.' Simplified and hybrid methods are used as well, such as payback period and discounted payback period.

   a. Preferred stock
   b. Gross profit
   c. Cash flow
   d. Capital budgeting

Chapter 21. Capital Budgeting and Cost Analysis

4. In finance, the _____ approach describes a method of valuing a project, company, or asset using the concepts of the time value of money. All future cash flows are estimated and discounted to give their present values. The discount rate used is generally the appropriate WACC, that reflects the risk of the cashflows.

   a. Discounted cash flow
   b. 3M Company
   c. Net present value
   d. Future value

5. _____ is the realization of an application idea, model, design, specification, standard, algorithm an _____ is a realization of a technical specification or algorithm as a program, software component, or other computer system. Many _____s may exist for a given specification or standard.

   a. AIG
   b. Implementation
   c. ABC Television Network
   d. AMEX

6. Simply put, _____ is the value of money figuring in a given amount of interest for a given amount of time. For example 100 dollars of todays money held for a year at 5 percent interest is worth 105 dollars, therefore 100 dollars paid now or 105 dollars paid exactly one year from now is the same amount of payment of money with that given intersest at that given amount of time. This notion dates at least to Martín de Azpilcueta of the School of Salamanca.

   a. Merck ' Co., Inc.
   b. Time value of money
   c. Competition law
   d. Collusion

7. _____ is the balance of the amounts of cash being received and paid by a business during a defined period of time, sometimes tied to a specific project. Measurement of _____ can be used

   - to evaluate the state or performance of a business or project.
   - to determine problems with liquidity. Being profitable does not necessarily mean being liquid. A company can fail because of a shortage of cash, even while profitable.
   - to project rate of returns. The time of _____s into and out of projects are used as inputs to financial models such as internal rate of return, and net present value.
   - to examine income or growth of a business when it is believed that accrual accounting concepts do not represent economic realities. Alternately, _____ can be used to 'validate' the net income generated by accrual accounting.

   _____ as a generic term may be used differently depending on context, and certain _____ definitions may be adapted by analysts and users for their own uses. Common terms include operating _____ and free _____.

a. Commercial paper
b. Controlling interest
c. Flow-through entity
d. Cash flow

8. The _____ is an expected return that the provider of capital plans to earn on their investment.

Capital (money) used for funding a business should earn returns for the capital providers who risk their capital. For an investment to be worthwhile, the expected return on capital must be greater than the _____.

a. Capital flight
b. Cost of capital
c. 3M Company
d. BMC Software, Inc.

9. Discounting is a financial mechanism in which a debtor obtains the right to delay payments to a creditor, for a defined period of time, in exchange for a charge or fee. Essentially, the party that owes money in the present purchases the right to delay the payment until some future date. The _____, or charge, is simply the difference between the original amount owed in the present and the amount that has to be paid in the future to settle the debt.
a. Discounting
b. Risk aversion
c. Discount factor
d. Discount

10. The _____ is an interest rate a central bank charges depository institutions that borrow reserves from it.

The term _____ has two meanings:

- the same as interest rate; the term 'discount' does not refer to the meaning of the word, but to the purpose of using the quantity, such as computations of present value, e.g. net present value or discounted cash flow

- the annual effective _____, which is the annual interest divided by the capital including that interest; this rate is lower than the interest rate; it corresponds to using the value after a year as the nominal value, and seeing the initial value as the nominal value minus a discount; it is used for Treasury Bills and similar financial instruments

The annual effective _____ is the annual interest divided by the capital including that interest, which is the interest rate divided by 100% plus the interest rate. It is the annual discount factor to be applied to the future cash flow, to find the discount, subtracted from a future value to find the value one year earlier.

Chapter 21. Capital Budgeting and Cost Analysis

For example, suppose there is a government bond that sells for $95 and pays $100 in a year's time.

a. Process time
b. Municipal bond
c. Convertible bond
d. Discount rate

11. _____ or net present worth (NPW) is defined as the total present value (PV) of a time series of cash flows. It is a standard method for using the time value of money to appraise long-term projects. Used for capital budgeting, and widely throughout economics, it measures the excess or shortfall of cash flows, in present value terms, once financing charges are met.

a. 3M Company
b. Net present value
c. Future value
d. Present value

12. _____ or economic opportunity loss is the value of the next best alternative foregone as the result of making a decision. _____ analysis is an important part of a company's decision-making processes but is not treated as an actual cost in any financial statement. The next best thing that a person can engage in is referred to as the _____ of doing the best thing and ignoring the next best thing to be done.

a. AIG
b. Inflation
c. ABC Television Network
d. Opportunity cost

13. _____ is the value on a given date of a future payment or series of future payments, discounted to reflect the time value of money and other factors such as investment risk. _____ calculations are widely used in business and economics to provide a means to compare cash flows at different times on a meaningful 'like to like' basis.

The most commonly applied model of the time value of money is compound interest.

a. Net present value
b. 3M Company
c. Future value
d. Present value

14. In finance, _____ also known as return on investment, rate of profit or sometimes just return, is the ratio of money gained or lost on an investment relative to the amount of money invested. The amount of money gained or lost may be referred to as interest, profit/loss, gain/loss, or net income/loss. The money invested may be referred to as the asset, capital, principal, or the cost basis of the investment.
   a. Capital employed
   b. Theoretical ex-rights price
   c. Debt to capital ratio
   d. Rate of return

15. An _____ is a term used in behavioral economics to describe those types of behaviors that impose costs on a person in the long-run that are not taken into account when making decisions in the present. Classical Economics discourages government from creating legislation that targets internalities, because it is assumed that the consumer takes these personal costs into account when paying for the good that causes the _____. For example, cigarettes should be taxed because of the negative consumption externalities that they impose, such as second-hand smoke, not because the smoker harms him or herself by smoking.
   a. Inventory turnover ratio
   b. Authorised capital
   c. Internality
   d. Operating budget

16. _____ is the study of how the variation (uncertainty) in the output of a mathematical model can be apportioned, qualitatively or quantitatively, to different sources of variation in the input of a model .

In more general terms uncertainty and sensitivity analyses investigate the robustness of a study when the study includes some form of mathematical modelling. While uncertainty analysis studies the overall uncertainty in the conclusions of the study, _____ tries to identify what source of uncertainty weights more on the study's conclusions.

   a. Free cash flow
   b. Kaizen
   c. Time to market
   d. Sensitivity analysis

17. The _____ is a capital budgeting metric used by firms to decide whether they should make investments. It is also called discounted cash flow rate of return (DCFROR) or rate of return (ROR.) It is an indicator of the efficiency or quality of an investment, as opposed to net present value (NPV), which indicates value or magnitude.

Chapter 21. Capital Budgeting and Cost Analysis

a. AIG
b. ABC Television Network
c. AMEX
d. Internal rate of return

18. _____ of something is, in finance, the adding together of interest or different investments over a period of time such as atoms (1 - the act or process of accruing; 2 - the amount that accrues.) It holds specific meanings in accounting and payroll.

_____, in accounting, describes the accounting method known as _____ basis, whereby revenues and expenses are recognized when they are accrued, i.e. accumulated (earned or incurred), regardless when the actual cash is received or paid out.

a. Earnings before interest, taxes, depreciation and amortization
b. Assets
c. Accounts receivable
d. Accrual

19. _____ is a method of accounting whereby economic activities (rather than cash flow) of financial events are considered, because of two complementary principles, which (together) determine the point, at which expenses and revenues are recognized. According to revenue recognition principle, revenues are realized when earned, whether or not they are received in cash.
a. Accrued revenue
b. Accrual
c. Accrual basis accounting
d. Earnings before interest, taxes, depreciation and amortization

20. The general definition of an _____ is an evaluation of a person, organization, system, process, project or product. _____s are performed to ascertain the validity and reliability of information; also to provide an assessment of a system's internal control. The goal of an _____ is to express an opinion on the person/organization/system (etc) in question, under evaluation based on work done on a test basis.
a. Assurance service
b. Audit regime
c. Institute of Chartered Accountants of India
d. Audit

110 *Chapter 21. Capital Budgeting and Cost Analysis*

21. In economic models, the _____ time frame assumes no fixed factors of production. Firms can enter or leave the marketplace, and the cost (and availability) of land, labor, raw materials, and capital goods can be assumed to vary. In contrast, in the short-run time frame, certain factors are assumed to be fixed, because there is not sufficient time for them to change.

   a. Long-run
   b. 3M Company
   c. BMC Software, Inc.
   d. Short-run

22. _____ is a process of attributing cost to particular cost centres. For example the wage of the driver of the purchasing department can be allocated to the purchasing department cost centre. It is not necessary to share the wage cost over several different cost centers.

   a. Cost allocation
   b. Cost of quality
   c. Variable cost
   d. Cost accounting

23. _____ is systematic determination of merit, worth, and significance of something or someone using criteria against a set of standards. _____ often is used to characterize and appraise subjects of interest in a wide range of human enterprises, including the arts, criminal justice, foundations and non-profit organizations, government, health care, and other human services.

   Depending on the topic of interest, there are professional groups which look to the quality and rigor of the _____ process.

   a. AIG
   b. AMEX
   c. ABC Television Network
   d. Evaluation

24. _____ in engineering is a method of manufacturing in which the entire production process is controlled by computer. The traditional separated process methods are joined through a computer by CIM. This integration allows that the processes exchange information with each other and they are able to initiate actions.

   a. 3M Company
   b. BMC Software, Inc.
   c. BNSF Railway
   d. Computer-integrated manufacturing

Chapter 21. Capital Budgeting and Cost Analysis

25. A _____, also client, buyer or purchaser is the buyer or user of the paid products of an individual or organization, mostly called the supplier or seller. This is typically through purchasing or renting goods or services.
   a. Customer
   b. 3M Company
   c. BNSF Railway
   d. BMC Software, Inc.

26. The phrase _____, according to the Organization for Economic Co-operation and Development, refers to 'creative work undertaken on a systematic basis in order to increase the stock of knowledge, including knowledge of man, culture and society, and the use of this stock of knowledge to devise new applications [sic]'

New product design and development is more than often a crucial factor in the survival of a company. In an industry that is fast changing, firms must continually revise their design and range of products. This is necessary due to continuous technology change and development as well as other competitors and the changing preference of customers.

   a. 3M Company
   b. BMC Software, Inc.
   c. BNSF Railway
   d. Research and development

27. In economics, _____ is a rise in the general level of prices of goods and services in an economy over a period of time. When the general price level rises, each unit of currency buys fewer goods and services; consequently, _____ is also a decline in the real value of money--a loss of purchasing power in the medium of exchange which is also the monetary unit of account in the economy. A chief measure of general price-level _____ is the general _____ rate, which is the percentage change in a general price index (normally the Consumer Price Index) over time.
   a. Inflation
   b. AIG
   c. Opportunity cost
   d. ABC Television Network

Chapter 22. Management Control Systems, Transfer Pricing, and Multinational Considerations

1. The _____ is a performance management tool which began as a concept for measuring whether the smaller-scale operational activities of a company are aligned with its larger-scale objectives in terms of vision and strategy.

By focusing not only on financial outcomes but also on the operational, marketing and developmental inputs to these, the _____ helps provide a more comprehensive view of a business, which in turn helps organizations act in their best long-term interests. This tool is also being used to address business response to climate change and greenhouse gas emissions.

   a. Best practice
   b. Management by objectives
   c. Trustee
   d. Balanced scorecard

2. A _____, also client, buyer or purchaser is the buyer or user of the paid products of an individual or organization, mostly called the supplier or seller. This is typically through purchasing or renting goods or services.
   a. BMC Software, Inc.
   b. BNSF Railway
   c. 3M Company
   d. Customer

3. In economics, _____ or _____ goods or real _____ refers to factors of production used to create goods or services that are not themselves significantly consumed (though they may depreciate) in the production process. _____ goods may be acquired with money or financial _____. In finance and accounting, _____ generally refers to financial wealth, especially that used to start or maintain a business.
   a. Screening
   b. Vyborg Appeal
   c. Capital
   d. Disclosure

4. _____ is the planning process used to determine whether a firm's long term investments such as new machinery, replacement machinery, new plants, new products, and research development projects are worth pursuing. It is budget for major capital, or investment, expenditures.

Many formal methods are used in _____, including the techniques such as

- Net present value
- Profitability index
- Internal rate of return
- Modified Internal Rate of Return
- Equivalent annuity

Chapter 22. Management Control Systems, Transfer Pricing, and Multinational Considerations

These methods use the incremental cash flows from each potential investment, or project. Techniques based on accounting earnings and accounting rules are sometimes used - though economists consider this to be improper - such as the accounting rate of return, and 'return on investment.' Simplified and hybrid methods are used as well, such as payback period and discounted payback period.

a. Preferred stock
b. Gross profit
c. Cash flow
d. Capital budgeting

5. _____ can be regarded as an outcome of mental processes (cognitive process) leading to the selection of a course of action among several alternatives. Every _____ process produces a final choice. The output can be an action or an opinion of choice.
a. Decision making
b. BNSF Railway
c. BMC Software, Inc.
d. 3M Company

6. In economics, business, retail, and accounting, a _____ is the value of money that has been used up to produce something, and hence is not available for use anymore. In economics, a _____ is an alternative that is given up as a result of a decision. In business, the _____ may be one of acquisition, in which case the amount of money expended to acquire it is counted as _____.
a. Cost of quality
b. Prime cost
c. Cost allocation
d. Cost

7. _____, in managerial economics is a form of cost accounting. It is a simplified model, useful for elementary instruction and for short-run decisions.

Cost-volume-profit (CVP) analysis expands the use of information provided by breakeven analysis.

a. Cost of quality
b. Fixed costs
c. Cost accounting
d. Cost-volume-profit analysis

Chapter 22. Management Control Systems, Transfer Pricing, and Multinational Considerations

8. _____ is a term that refers both to:

- a formal discipline used to help appraise, or assess, the case for a project or proposal, which itself is a process known as project appraisal; and
- an informal approach to making decisions of any kind.

Under both definitions the process involves, whether explicitly or implicitly, weighing the total expected costs against the total expected benefits of one or more actions in order to choose the best or most profitable option. The formal process is often referred to as either CBA (_____) or BCost-benefit analysis

A hallmark of CBA is that all benefits and all costs are expressed in money terms, and are adjusted for the time value of money, so that all flows of benefits and flows of project costs over time (which tend to occur at different points in time) are expressed on a common basis in terms of their 'e;present value.'e; Closely related, but slightly different, formal techniques include Cost-effectiveness analysis, Economic impact analysis, Fiscal impact analysis and Social Return on Investment(SROI) analysis. The latter builds upon the logic of _____, but differs in that it is explicitly designed to inform the practical decision-making of enterprise managers and investors focused on optimising their social and environmental impacts.

   a. BMC Software, Inc.
   b. BNSF Railway
   c. Cost-benefit analysis
   d. 3M Company

9. An _____ is a classification used for business units within an enterprise. The essential element of an _____ is that it is treated as a unit which is measured against its use of capital, as opposed to a cost or profit center, which are measured against raw costs or profits.

The advantage of this form of measurement is that it tends to be more encompassing, since it accounts for all uses of capital.

   a. Investment center
   b. ABC Television Network
   c. AMEX
   d. AIG

10. _____ is one of the four Ps of the marketing mix. The other three aspects are product, promotion, and place. It is also a key variable in microeconomic price allocation theory.

Chapter 22. Management Control Systems, Transfer Pricing, and Multinational Considerations

a. Cost-plus pricing
b. Target costing
c. Pricing
d. Price

11. _____s are parts of a corporation that directly add to its profit.

A _____ manager is held accountable for both revenues, and costs (expenses), and therefore, profits. What this means in terms of managerial responsibilities is that the manager has to drive the sales revenue generating activities which leads to cash inflows and at the same time control the cost (cash outflows) causing activities.

a. Profit center
b. Cost management
c. Cost driver
d. Contribution margin

12. _____ refers to the pricing of contributions (assets, tangible and intangible, services, and funds) transferred within an organization. For example, goods from the production division may be sold to the marketing division, or goods from a parent company may be sold to a foreign subsidiary. Since the prices are set within an organization (i.e. controlled), the typical market mechanisms that establish prices for such transactions between third parties may not apply.
a. Transactional Net Margin Method
b. Pricing
c. Transfer Pricing
d. Price

13. A _____ is an economy based on the division of labor in which the prices of goods and services are determined in a free price system set by supply and demand. This is often contrasted with a planned economy, in which a central government determines the price of goods and services using a fixed price system. Market economies are contrasted with mixed economy where the price system is not entirely free but under some government control that is not extensive enough to constitute a planned economy.
a. Market economy
b. BNSF Railway
c. 3M Company
d. BMC Software, Inc.

14. _____ in economics and business is the result of an exchange and from that trade we assign a numerical monetary value to a good, service or asset. If Alice trades Bob 4 apples for an orange, the _____ of an orange is 4 apples. Inversely, the _____ of an apple is 1/4 oranges.

a. Price discrimination
b. Transactional Net Margin Method
c. Price
d. Discounts and allowances

15. _____s are expenses that change in proportion to the activity of a business. In other words, _____ is the sum of marginal costs. It can also be considered normal costs.
    a. Fixed costs
    b. Cost accounting
    c. Quality costs
    d. Variable cost

16. An _____ is a term used in behavioral economics to describe those types of behaviors that impose costs on a person in the long-run that are not taken into account when making decisions in the present. Classical Economics discourages government from creating legislation that targets internalities, because it is assumed that the consumer takes these personal costs into account when paying for the good that causes the _____. For example, cigarettes should be taxed because of the negative consumption externalities that they impose, such as second-hand smoke, not because the smoker harms him or herself by smoking.
    a. Inventory turnover ratio
    b. Authorised capital
    c. Operating budget
    d. Internality

17. The _____ is the United States federal government agency that collects taxes and enforces the internal revenue laws. It is an agency within the U.S. Dept of the treasury responsible for interpretation and application of Federal tax law. The official U.S. Treasury regulations provide (in part):

The _____ is a bureau of the Department of the Treasury under the immediate direction of the Commissioner of Internal Revenue.

   a. Use tax
   b. Income tax
   c. Indirect tax
   d. Internal Revenue Service

Chapter 23. Performance Measurement, Compensation, and Multinational Considerations

1. The _____ is a performance management tool which began as a concept for measuring whether the smaller-scale operational activities of a company are aligned with its larger-scale objectives in terms of vision and strategy.

By focusing not only on financial outcomes but also on the operational, marketing and developmental inputs to these, the _____ helps provide a more comprehensive view of a business, which in turn helps organizations act in their best long-term interests. This tool is also being used to address business response to climate change and greenhouse gas emissions.

   a. Management by objectives
   b. Best practice
   c. Trustee
   d. Balanced scorecard

2. _____ is the process whereby an organization establishes the parameters within which programs, investments, and acquisitions are reaching the desired results. Performance Reference Model of the Federal Enterprise Architecture, 2005.

This process of measuring performance often requires the use of statistical evidence to determine progress toward specific defined organizational objectives.

There are many types of measurements.

   a. Management by exception
   b. Trustee
   c. Management by objectives
   d. Performance measurement

3. Total _____ is a method of Accounting cost which entails the full cost of manufacturing or providing a service. This includes not just the costs of materials and labour, but also of all manufacturing overheads (whether e;fixede; or e;variablee;.) One of the main reasons for absorbing overheads into the cost of units is for inventory valuation purposes.
   a. AMEX
   b. ABC Television Network
   c. Absorption costing
   d. AIG

4. In finance, _____ also known as return on investment, rate of profit or sometimes just return, is the ratio of money gained or lost on an investment relative to the amount of money invested. The amount of money gained or lost may be referred to as interest, profit/loss, gain/loss, or net income/loss. The money invested may be referred to as the asset, capital, principal, or the cost basis of the investment.

Chapter 23. Performance Measurement, Compensation, and Multinational Considerations

a. Debt to capital ratio
b. Theoretical ex-rights price
c. Capital employed
d. Rate of return

5. In corporate finance, _____ or _____ is an estimate of true economic profit after making corrective adjustments to GAAP accounting, including deducting the opportunity cost of equity capital. _____ can be measured as Net Operating Profit After Taxes(or NOPAT) less the money cost of capital. _____ is similar in nature to that of calculating another financial performance measure - Residual Income , however, there are a few complexities involved with coming up with the elements for calculating _____ over RI such as the myriad adjustments that might be made to NOPAT before it is suitable for the formula below.

a. International Monetary Fund
b. Outsourcing
c. Economic value added
d. Internal control

6. In economics, _____ or _____ goods or real _____ refers to factors of production used to create goods or services that are not themselves significantly consumed (though they may depreciate) in the production process. _____ goods may be acquired with money or financial _____. In finance and accounting, _____ generally refers to financial wealth, especially that used to start or maintain a business.

a. Capital
b. Disclosure
c. Screening
d. Vyborg Appeal

7. In economics, business, retail, and accounting, a _____ is the value of money that has been used up to produce something, and hence is not available for use anymore. In economics, a _____ is an alternative that is given up as a result of a decision. In business, the _____ may be one of acquisition, in which case the amount of money expended to acquire it is counted as _____.

a. Cost of quality
b. Cost allocation
c. Prime cost
d. Cost

8. The _____ is an expected return that the provider of capital plans to earn on their investment.

Capital (money) used for funding a business should earn returns for the capital providers who risk their capital. For an investment to be worthwhile, the expected return on capital must be greater than the _____.

Chapter 23. Performance Measurement, Compensation, and Multinational Considerations

a. 3M Company
b. Capital flight
c. BMC Software, Inc.
d. Cost of capital

9. _____ refers to the additional value of a commodity over the cost of commodities used to produce it from the previous stage of production. An example is the price of gasoline at the pump over the price of the oil in it. In national accounts used in macroeconomics, it refers to the contribution of the factors of production, i.e., land, labor, and capital goods, to raising the value of a product and corresponds to the incomes received by the owners of these factors.

a. Supply-side economics
b. 3M Company
c. Value added
d. Minimum wage

10. In business, operating margin, operating income margin, operating profit margin or _____ is the ratio of operating income (operating profit in the UK) divided by net sales, usually presented in percent.

$$\text{Operating margin} = \left(\frac{\text{Operating income}}{\text{Revenue}}\right)$$

(Relevant figures in italics)

$$\text{Operating margin} = \left(\frac{6,318}{24,088}\right) = \underline{26.23\%}$$

It is a measurement of what proportion of a company's revenue is left over, before taxes and other indirect costs (such as rent, bonus, interest, etc.), after paying for variable costs of production as wages, raw materials, etc. A good operating margin is needed for a company to be able to pay for its fixed costs, such as interest on debt.

a. Total revenue share
b. Return on sales
c. Diluted Earnings Per Share
d. Debt service coverage ratio

11. A _____ is the pinnacle activity involved in selling products or services in return for money or other compensation. It is an act of completion of a commercial activity.

A _____ is completed by the seller, the owner of the goods.

Chapter 23. Performance Measurement, Compensation, and Multinational Considerations

a. Maturity
b. High yield stock
c. Tertiary sector of economy
d. Sale

12. A _____ is a fixed point of time in the future at which point certain processes will be evaluated or assumed to end. It is necessary in an accounting, finance or risk management regime to assign such a fixed horizon time so that alternatives can be evaluated for performance over the same period of time. A _____ is a physical impossibility in the real world.

a. 3M Company
b. BNSF Railway
c. BMC Software, Inc.
d. Time horizon

13. In business and accounting, _____ are everything of value that is owned by a person or company. It is a claim on the property your income of a borrower. The balance sheet of a firm records the monetary value of the _____ owned by the firm.

a. Accrual basis accounting
b. Earnings before interest, taxes, depreciation and amortization
c. Accounts receivable
d. Assets

14. In accounting, _____ or carrying value is the value of an asset according to its balance sheet account balance. For assets, the value is based on the original cost of the asset less any depreciation, amortization or impairment costs made against the asset. Traditionally, a company's _____ is its total assets minus intangible assets and liabilities.

a. Generally accepted accounting principles
b. Matching principle
c. Depreciation
d. Book value

15. In economic models, the _____ time frame assumes no fixed factors of production. Firms can enter or leave the marketplace, and the cost (and availability) of land, labor, raw materials, and capital goods can be assumed to vary. In contrast, in the short-run time frame, certain factors are assumed to be fixed, because there is not sufficient time for them to change.

a. BMC Software, Inc.
b. 3M Company
c. Short-run
d. Long-run

16. _____ describes the situation when output from (or information about the result of) an event or phenomenon in the past will influence the same event/phenomenon in the present or future. When an event is part of a chain of cause-and-effect that forms a circuit or loop, then the event is said to 'feed back' into itself.

_____ is also a synonym for:

- _____ Signal; the information about the initial event that is the basis for subsequent modification of the event.
- _____ Loop; the causal path that leads from the initial generation of the _____ signal to the subsequent modification of the event.

_____ is a mechanism, process or signal that is looped back to control a system within itself. Such a loop is called a _____ loop.

a. Controllable
b. BMC Software, Inc.
c. Feedback
d. 3M Company

17. In economics and sociology, an _____ is any factor (financial or non-financial) that enables or motivates a particular course of action, or counts as a reason for preferring one choice to the alternatives. It is an expectation that encourages people to behave in a certain way. Since human beings are purposeful creatures, the study of _____ structures is central to the study of all economic activity (both in terms of individual decision-making and in terms of co-operation and competition within a larger institutional structure.)
a. ABC Television Network
b. Incentive
c. AMEX
d. AIG

18. _____ is a concept that denotes the precise probability of specific eventualities. Technically, the notion of _____ is independent from the notion of value and, as such, eventualities may have both beneficial and adverse consequences. However, in general usage the convention is to focus only on potential negative impact to some characteristic of value that may arise from a future event.

Chapter 23. Performance Measurement, Compensation, and Multinational Considerations

a. Risk adjusted return on capital
b. Discount factor
c. Discounting
d. Risk

19. _____ is the process of comparing the cost, cycle time, productivity, or quality of a specific process or method to another that is widely considered to be an industry standard or best practice. Essentially, _____ provides a snapshot of the performance of your business and helps you understand where you are in relation to a particular standard. The result is often a business case for making changes in order to make improvements.

a. Benchmarking
b. 3M Company
c. Strategic business unit
d. BMC Software, Inc.

20. _____ is systematic determination of merit, worth, and significance of something or someone using criteria against a set of standards. _____ often is used to characterize and appraise subjects of interest in a wide range of human enterprises, including the arts, criminal justice, foundations and non-profit organizations, government, health care, and other human services.

Depending on the topic of interest, there are professional groups which look to the quality and rigor of the _____ process.

a. AIG
b. AMEX
c. Evaluation
d. ABC Television Network

21. In options, the _____ is a key variable in a derivatives contract between two parties. Where the contract requires delivery of the underlying instrument, the trade will be at the _____, regardless of the spot price (market price) of the underlying instrument at that time.

Definition - The fixed price at which the owner of an option can purchase, in the case of a call in the case of a put, the underlying security or commodity.

a. BMC Software, Inc.
b. 3M Company
c. Put option
d. Strike price

Chapter 23. Performance Measurement, Compensation, and Multinational Considerations

22. _____ in economics and business is the result of an exchange and from that trade we assign a numerical monetary value to a good, service or asset. If Alice trades Bob 4 apples for an orange, the _____ of an orange is 4 apples. Inversely, the _____ of an apple is 1/4 oranges.
    a. Price discrimination
    b. Discounts and allowances
    c. Transactional Net Margin Method
    d. Price

23. A _____ is a fungible, negotiable instrument representing financial value. they are broadly categorized into debt securities (such as banknotes, bonds and debentures), and equity securities; e.g., common stocks. The company or other entity issuing the _____ is called the issuer.
    a. BMC Software, Inc.
    b. Tracking stock
    c. 3M Company
    d. Security

24. The U.S. _____ is an independent agency of the United States government which holds primary responsibility for enforcing the federal securities laws and regulating the securities industry, the nation's stock and options exchanges, and other electronic securities markets. The SEC was created by section 4 of the Securities Exchange Act of 1934 (now codified as 15 U.S.C. ÂÂ§ 78d and commonly referred to as the 1934 Act.)
    a. BMC Software, Inc.
    b. 3M Company
    c. Securities and Exchange Commission
    d. BNSF Railway

25. In finance, an _____ is a contract between a buyer and a seller that gives the buyer the right--but not the obligation-- to buy or to sell a particular asset (the underlying asset) at a later time at an agreed price. In return for granting the _____, the seller collects a payment (the premium) from the buyer. A call _____ gives the buyer the right to buy the underlying asset; a put _____ gives the buyer of the _____ the right to sell the underlying asset.
    a. AIG
    b. AMEX
    c. Option
    d. ABC Television Network

Chapter 1
1. d	2. d	3. c	4. c	5. d	6. a	7. d	8. d	9. a	10. b
11. d	12. a	13. a	14. b	15. d	16. c	17. d	18. a	19. d	20. b
21. d	22. a	23. d	24. b	25. a	26. d	27. d	28. d	29. d	30. b
31. a	32. d	33. a	34. a						

Chapter 2
1. b	2. b	3. d	4. d	5. b	6. d	7. d	8. b	9. b	10. d
11. d	12. d	13. a	14. d	15. d	16. b	17. d	18. d	19. c	20. a
21. d	22. d	23. d							

Chapter 3
1. c	2. d	3. a	4. d	5. c	6. d	7. a	8. d	9. a	10. d
11. d	12. d	13. d	14. a	15. d	16. c				

Chapter 4
1. d	2. d	3. a	4. d	5. a	6. d	7. d	8. c	9. d	10. d
11. b	12. d	13. b	14. a	15. d					

Chapter 5
1. b	2. d	3. d	4. d	5. b	6. d	7. a	8. d	9. a	10. b
11. d	12. d	13. d							

Chapter 6
1. d	2. c	3. d	4. c	5. d	6. d	7. d	8. d	9. d	10. c
11. d	12. c	13. a	14. d	15. c	16. c	17. b	18. c	19. d	20. d
21. a	22. a	23. c							

Chapter 7
1. d	2. d	3. b	4. d	5. d	6. d	7. b	8. d	9. a	10. a
11. b	12. d	13. c	14. b	15. a					

Chapter 8
1. c	2. b	3. c	4. a	5. d	6. d	7. d	8. a	9. b	10. b

Chapter 9
1. d	2. d	3. d	4. d	5. d	6. d	7. c	8. d	9. d	10. d
11. c	12. b	13. b	14. a	15. a					

Chapter 10
1. d	2. b	3. d	4. d	5. d	6. d	7. d	8. b	9. c	10. d
11. d	12. a	13. d	14. c						

Chapter 11
1. b	2. a	3. b	4. d	5. b	6. a	7. d	8. b	9. c	10. a
11. a	12. d	13. d	14. a	15. d	16. a	17. d	18. d		

ANSWER KEY

Chapter 12
1. d 2. d 3. c 4. d 5. c 6. d 7. d 8. b 9. c 10. d
11. a 12. d 13. d 14. d 15. d 16. a 17. a 18. c 19. b 20. a
21. b 22. d 23. d 24. c 25. b 26. b 27. d 28. d 29. d 30. d
31. d

Chapter 13
1. c 2. d 3. d 4. d 5. d 6. d 7. d 8. d 9. d 10. b
11. d 12. c 13. b

Chapter 14
1. d 2. d 3. b 4. c 5. b 6. a 7. d 8. a 9. c

Chapter 15
1. d 2. d 3. d 4. a 5. d 6. c 7. d

Chapter 16
1. c 2. c 3. d 4. d 5. c 6. d

Chapter 17
1. c

Chapter 18
1. d 2. b 3. d 4. d 5. d

Chapter 19
1. d 2. c 3. d 4. d 5. d 6. a 7. d 8. a 9. b 10. d
11. d 12. c 13. d 14. c 15. d 16. c 17. c 18. d 19. d 20. c
21. a 22. a 23. c

Chapter 20
1. a 2. c 3. b 4. d 5. c 6. b 7. b 8. d 9. d 10. d
11. d 12. d 13. d 14. d 15. a 16. d 17. a 18. d 19. d 20. b

Chapter 21
1. d 2. d 3. d 4. a 5. b 6. b 7. d 8. b 9. d 10. d
11. b 12. d 13. d 14. d 15. c 16. d 17. d 18. d 19. c 20. d
21. a 22. a 23. d 24. d 25. a 26. d 27. a

Chapter 22
1. d 2. d 3. c 4. d 5. a 6. d 7. d 8. c 9. a 10. c
11. a 12. c 13. a 14. c 15. d 16. d 17. d

Chapter 23

1. d	2. d	3. c	4. d	5. c	6. a	7. d	8. d	9. c	10. b
11. d	12. d	13. d	14. d	15. d	16. c	17. b	18. d	19. a	20. c
21. d	22. d	23. d	24. c	25. c					

www.ingramcontent.com/pod-product-compliance
Lightning Source LLC
Chambersburg PA
CBHW082046230426
43670CB00016B/2793